D0939129

12/8/2016

Kathie -

Thank you for being a part of my story. As an example of cheerful giving and sincerity of heart, I look up to you for so many reasons and think you are wonderful. ♡

Thank you for feeding us and giving us shelter and kind warmth in a time of repair + restoration - I appreciate your influence and your friendship.

This book is my faith story. It's why I call Jesus my friend and Savior. Maybe we can talk about it someday. I hope it touches your heart or encourages you in some way as you read it. Love always -

Davida Blanton

SWEET REVELATION

SEEING AND BEING THE UNVEILED ARM OF GOD

DAVIDA BLANTON

ILLUSTRATIONS BY KIMBERLY WASSON TENER

WESTBOW
PRESS®
A DIVISION OF THOMAS NELSON
& ZONDERVAN

WestBow Press books may be ordered through booksellers or by contacting:

WestBow Press
A Division of Thomas Nelson & Zondervan
1663 Liberty Drive
Bloomington, IN 47403
www.westbowpress.com
1 (866) 928-1240

ISBN: 978-1-5127-0694-9 (sc)
ISBN: 978-1-5127-0695-6 (hc)
ISBN: 978-1-5127-0693-2 (e)

Library of Congress Control Number: 2015912664

Print information available on the last page.

WestBow Press rev. date: 10/20/2015

For you, the reader

That you might see Jesus in <u>your</u> story

CONTENTS

ACKNOWLEDGEMENTS

My Mom, Linda Duffield- You taught me how to read and write, so I think you deserve some serious credit for this! I hope that reading it will bring you joy. You are also the one that led me to Jesus. Thank you. Praise Him for all I have become, and all that I am yet to be. You showed me what it means to trust God *in* everything and *for* everything. I want nothing else for my life. I'm so grateful every day for you and Dad. All you did for us kids, all you taught us. We are blessed beyond measure. I can't wait until we're *all* together, *really* together, again. When our Lord will wipe every tear from our eyes. And there will be no more death, nor crying, neither shall there be any more pain. Revelation 21:4

Mr. Robert Riggins- My greatest inspiration with regard to my writing. Thank you for encouraging me to learn all I can and to express myself with boldness. Thank you for playing beautiful music in your classroom; it gave me an atmosphere in which to vibrantly thrive. I have never ceased to pray that you will see the glory light of Jesus Christ and that you will abide in its warmth for eternity.

My husband, Mark Blanton- You are a picture of Christ's love for me, and that will wow me for the rest of my life. Thank you for believing in me and for accepting me so unconditionally- and for being really cool about this book project. Dreaming with you never gets old. I love listening for the trumpet with you. I love worshipping God by your side. I'm glad He joined us together. Matthew 19:6: "So they are no longer two, but one flesh. What therefore God has joined together, let not man put asunder."

Mary Jane Hayes Curling- My mentor and my sister in Jesus. You taught me what it means to be a Godly woman. Thank you for making me see my gifts all those times, and for loving me like a daughter. I was privileged to know you and I always wanted to make you proud. I miss you and cannot wait to be with you again in the Kingdom of God.

Cecil and Connie Blanton- You give and give and you give some more. You have done so much for me. Thank you for all the sacrifices you've made, to allow me to live in comfort. I do not take it for granted, nor will I ever. Thank you for raising up a good man for me to marry and to love for all my days. Your legacy of love and giving will continue in our children. Your grandchildren. And in their children's children, should the Lord tarry. I will always love you.

Kelly Eiseman- You told me not to put off writing this book. That was great advice! I look up to you and I love you. I think you are brave. You honor me with your special friendship. I pray God's blessing and favor upon you and your family.

Donald Miller- It's because of you that I decided to tell my story. You inspire me to make my life a story worth telling. I don't want to waste a single day. Thank you for teaching me how to live deliberately, how to live deep, and to suck out all the marrow of life. And that sharing my soul with the world can actually be a good thing.

CHAPTER 1

WHY THIS BOOK EXISTS

I was the kid who would rather make up a story than read one. I've never disliked reading, but if given the choice to read or to write, I'd rather write. Ever since learning how to form my alphabet letters, I've enjoyed expressing myself through writing. As a young girl, I delighted in making cards and writing letters for people. It was how I could say what I really meant. So many times I just couldn't say what I really felt by speaking it. But I always could by writing it down.

My mother taught me first and second grade at home. No doubt she recognized my eagerness to write, early on. She encouraged my enjoyment of making cards and writing notes to family and friends. She once gave me a small plastic card maker that I could use to make cards from paper. It had removable plates with raised shapes on them- like rainbows, flowers and hearts. I could rub crayons over the shapes to make my cards look just how I wanted. That little gadget served me very well. I wore it out. I must have made hundreds of cards with it. Each card's outside was custom-colored by my own hands, and inside was custom-written by my own heart.

1

When I was six years old, my mother gave me a special writing project. It was a meaningful assignment, one which I completed happily and eagerly. I was charged with the task of communicating some things about American liberty, in a written report, to any person of my choice. I was required to read about symbols of American liberty and then describe them to my chosen recipient. At the time, our family lived at a Bible school for adult students preparing to be Christian pastors and missionaries. I knew many of the students, as we lived right on campus and my father worked in the dining hall. I was often there in his big kitchen, helping him or waiting for him, and I would talk with the students in the dining room as they ate their meals. One of the young students in the Bible school was Sujaya.

Sujaya had come from India to study Bible. He had the darkest skin I'd ever seen. His eyes were huge, and to me they looked black. They were always smiling, and so was his mouth. Sujaya's laugh was loud and a little bit frightening, but I loved hearing it and seeing his ivory teeth glisten as his mouth broke into a wide smile, shiny and pearly, in marked contrast against the extremely dark complexion of his face. Sujaya stood out to me far more than any other student. Not only did he have a strikingly unique appearance, but he was from a place far away, which naturally intrigued me. I would sit with him and listen intently as he talked to me about India. I was fascinated by all he told me.

When it came time to write my report about American liberty, I knew that Sujaya was the one I was supposed to write it for. I wanted him to know about America the way he had told me about India. I wanted him to experience American freedom. I worked hard to gather facts from various books- facts about the American bald eagle, the Statue of Liberty, the Liberty Bell, and Old Glory itself. In doing so, I learned about these symbols of American freedom. I wrote about what they represented to Americans, what they meant to me, and why I was proud of my country. What I wrote was special to Sujaya. I knew that because he looked me directly in the eyes and told me so, in his big billowing gentle voice.

What I wrote was special to me, too. I loved Sujaya and my writing was an expression of that love.

Just as I wrote especially for Sujaya as a little girl, I write now to YOU. This book is really a letter- my personal letter- to you. It is my story. I don't tell it because I want to talk about myself. I don't write it to convince you that I am cool or that you should live your life like mine. I tell you my story because I want your life to be free. Not free of problems, but free of worry, fear, guilt and shame. I want you to dwell in a powerful liberty, all the time. This liberty I know is not a civil liberty like I wrote about for Sujaya. It is liberty *of soul.*

I didn't grow up planning to write a book. In high school I wrote some short stories, one of which I entered in a contest and won. But it was really just for fun. In college I wrote an essay that granted me a scholarship and a special place on stage at the annual awards ceremony. That was pretty cool. But it was really just for money. In 2005 I discovered the world of blogging and thought it was extraordinary. I began reading blogs that inspired and educated me. I started my own blog titled *Paint the Truth.* Only my friends and family read *Paint the Truth.* It was an outlet for me to share with them what was on my mind and what was going on in my life. I did not predict that my writing would ever reach past the scope of that little blog.

Then in the summer of 2010, my friend Val gave me a book written by Donald Miller, titled *A Million Miles in a Thousand Years: What I Learned While Editing My Life.*[1] It was different from other books I had read, because it was like I could hear the writer's voice, like he was talking to me on the phone or across a cafe table. That doesn't usually happen when I read. The author's words compelled me to consider my own life story, to ask myself what kind of story I was living out. I began to imagine what it would be like if my life were acted out as a movie. I thought, "What is the main theme of *my* story? What would *my* movie be about? If someone were watching my whole life in two dimensions on a flat screen TV, what would that look like?" And the answer came quickly:

SWEET REVELATION.

Sweet revelation is what I call it when I get to see a little bit of what God is really like. It is my most dominant recurring theme. I keep seeing little bits of God, and every time I see Him He is bright, warm, beautiful. And perfect.

I'm not talking about one vision or a single isolated apparition of God. Nor am I referring to some dream I keep having that's the same every time I dream it. No. My sweet revelation has been a series of life events-- situations that have put me in places where I was able to "see" God. Specific times that I have been in some serious spiritual or physical trouble, and God came to my rescue-- each time in a different way, but each time there and each time strong. As though the setting of my life is an ocean, and He is a ship Captain who opens His giant bin of life preservers every time I start to drown. Each life preserver is a different shape and a different color, but perfectly designed to keep me afloat, and then He pulls me in and I can see some new part of Him that I didn't see before I grabbed the preserver. Like the preserver is connected to His character. And when I reach Him in those moments of utter panic, He calms me. He lifts me up into His big mercy ship and guides me into the Captain's cabin where it's warm and dry, where He has a blanket and a delicious warm nourishing meal for me, which is the very Word spoken from His mouth. And we regale the tale together, of how I would have been a goner if I hadn't seen Him and grabbed that preserver. And then I tell him "thank you" and He tells me "I love you" and I go to sleep in a warm bed without fear of what tomorrow will bring. Even if we're sailing through a horrific storm. If I awaken to hear the wind outside the ship, I know I am OK. Because I know that my capable Captain can't make a mistake. His ship can't sink, and if I *do* get tossed overboard for some reason- or if I *JUMP* overboard like a big idiot because I forget that the ship is the safest place to be- well then, I might flail around in the water awhile and it might be too dark for me to see Him, but if I really just focus for a minute, I see Him still there, with yet another life preserver. And I grab it. And He pulls me in again to safety.

And this continues like a cycle. This is what my "walk" with God has been like. Like a journey on a ship, with an occasional swim in very turbulent water, salty and scary and cold. But He really is right there, and tells me to *quit jumping overboard-* because He's got me covered. If I forget that again, His bin of life preservers is bottomless, and He'll be right there again to throw me one. But always when He does, grabbing on to it is up to me.

Going back to that summer of 2010, while reading Donald Miller's book, I thought, "How crazy would it be for *me* to write a book?" That question was usually followed in my mind with another question, "Who would even read it if I did?" So I pushed the thought out of my mind for a time; but it was always still there, somewhere in the back.

During that time and throughout the coming months, I endured a time of tragic struggle. The kind of struggle that brings you all the way down to a beaten pulp spiritually, the kind that changes you for good. Much of this book is my recounting of what happened in me during that time. It was during that painful process that writing became more to me than just a hobby. It became my primary method of processing all that I was going through. A therapy of sorts. A means of interpreting thoughts, emotions, and major life lessons that I was learning. Toward the end of that hard stretch of months, I was challenged by several different people- at isolated times- to put my writing ability to better use than I had been, to do something meaningful with it. It was obvious that I had a story to tell. One worth telling, one that *should* be told, because maybe it could make a difference for someone else who might be facing turbulent high seas. I was saddened by the fact that I didn't write letters much anymore. "What's keeping me from writing all this down?" I asked myself. One answer to that question was my job. My job was keeping me from having the time and concentration that writing a book would require. So I put the thought out of my mind again, and just did my job instead.

Shortly thereafter, my job was removed from the picture. I felt as if my work rug was being pulled out from under me. But to my surprise, I found myself still standing, and standing strong! As unexpected as that was, it seemed that God was prompting me, saying, "Now you can write that book you keep thinking about!" I sensed that it was one of those "now or never" times, and I really wanted to write. I attended the Global Leadership Summit in August 2011, an international conference held in Chicago but fed via satellite to locations all around the United States and the world. Many gifted individuals come to the Summit to teach people how to be leaders in their communities. The conference lasted two days. During that time, God confirmed to me through THREE different speakers that I needed to tell my story to whomever would listen to it, because it just might make a powerful difference for somebody somewhere. I knew I'd been given the ability to deliver an important message, and that it was time to just do it.

So here it is.

And it's for *you*.

Maybe you're reading this and you don't believe God is real. Maybe you are unsure whether He is real or not. Perhaps you *want* to believe in Him, but you aren't convinced He isn't some fairy tale. Maybe you *DO* believe God is real, but you don't care for Him much, for whatever reason. Maybe you've felt all along

He is real, but you are angry with Him. Or maybe you're reading this and can say that you love Him more than yourself; He is your whole life. Wherever you are concerning God right now, I invite you to relax and just rest easy as you read this book. It is not my attempt to convince you of the rightness of any particular religion. It is not an attempt to "wow" you with my experiences, or even to prove the existence of God. It is simply my narrative, some life memoirs, recorded on these pages with the specific intent to give you a clear window through which to peer. A window into sweet revelation in my life, but also in yours. As you read my story, I hope that you *consider your own*. Contemplate your own experiences, all the unique triumphs and trials that you've encountered in the rough sea that is this life. Consider the possibility that God has been there right with you all along, keeping you from drowning, wanting to show you Himself if you would only see Him.

Revelation 19:10 tells us that the substance, the very essence, of the truth revealed by Jesus is the spirit of all prophecy. It is the vital breath, the inspiration of all God-breathed preaching and all true interpretation of God's divine will and purpose. My purpose and *your* purpose. The truth that Jesus reveals to us all is really the message of this book. I have asked Jesus to show you His radiant light, in my true story and in yours.

CHAPTER 2

AN ARM REVEALED

"Who has believed our message?
And to whom has the arm of the Lord been revealed?"
Isaiah 53:1 (NIV)

When you hear the word "reveal", what first comes to your mind? Think about that word for a moment: *REVEAL*. If something is "revealed" to you, what does that mean really?

When I think of the word "reveal", I imagine a pair of eyes. Open eyes. Eyes that see something they could not see before. Now you don't see it...now you *DO!*

I find it interesting to learn the origins of words. If that makes me a word nerd, so be it. The word "reveal" is at least 700 years old and is a combination of the Latin prefix *re-*, meaning "opposite of", and the Latin verb *velare*, meaning "to cover". From *velare* comes the noun *velum*, which gives us our English word "veil".[1] Etymologically, then, a "revelation" is an unveiling. To *reveal* something is to uncover it, to unveil it. When a covering is removed, something is exposed. Something that was not visible before is now visible, perhaps only in part, or perhaps entirely. Ready to be seen with seeing eyes.

9

EYES THAT SEE

Human eyesight completely fascinates me. Our eyes are said to be the "windows into our souls". They are also our windows *out*, to the world. When we speak about seeing something, we don't always have a full grasp of everything that entails. We don't think about the *physiology* of vision very much; we just take it for granted most of the time. But it's actually quite an impressive phenomenon.

This miraculous process begins in your body at a fraction of the instant when light, *traveling 299,792, 458 meters per second,* hits your cornea and is focused through the lens. The light then travels through the gelatinous pool that is the vitreous, all the way to the flat-screen retina at the back of your eye. At the retina, special cells called rods and cones carefully detect the brightness and color of the light passing through them, and they immediately convert that light into electrochemical signals which travel along a nerve bundle called the optic nerve. From there the signals ride the nerve highway fast lane to the back of your brain, where the signals are interpreted as an image. The brain then perceives the image formed from the reflected light that bounced off whatever it was you looked at. And that's when you actually "see" the thing. And this happens automatically, *autonomically,* in about 1/1000 of a second. [2]

Truly incredible.

But in order for this process to occur successfully, *light* must enter the eye. That light must reach the retina and must be changed into a message the brain can interpret. If one of these steps is not carried out as it should be, vision will not take place. Light is the key to seeing. That's why we can't see anything in total darkness.

Visual *perspective* is also a factor in how we see what we see. Objects are perceived to be a certain color, shape, depth, or distance away. Sometimes perspective is skewed. A person's ability to see an object for what it really is depends on the condition of his eyes and nerves and on his proximity to the object. Likewise, the angle of his location in relation to the object plays a part in how he sees it. It is entirely possible for you and me to be standing together in a well-lit room, facing an object, and one of us sees the entire object clearly, but the other does not. Your eyesight would be inhibited if you could not open your eyes, or if they were covered, or if the light could not reach your retina for any other reason. Similarly, if my optic nerve were impaired, there would be no superhighway to conduct the electrical signal to tell my brain what my eye is seeing. If I were standing several feet from the object and you were closer to it, you would probably see it better than I would. It's possible that the object could be there all along, and neither of us would see it at all, if something kept us from seeing it.

Now let's think about this in the context of our spiritual "eyesight" and the condition of our "spiritual eyes".

I believe I have a spirit and you have a spirit. I believe *every one of us* is part spirit. We are not body and mind only; there is more to us than that. The spirit part of us is not seen by human eyes. But God sees it. The spirit part of us lives forever. It was given to us by God, just as He gave us our bodies and minds. God Himself is Spirit (John 4:24). Our spirits are connected to the Spirit of God their Maker. Connected, but not equal. God's Spirit is perfect, holy, *sinless*. Our spirits are tainted, stained by corrupted flesh, flawed by our sinful acts (Jude 1:22). Our sins separate our spirits from God's Spirit. Our sins have caused our souls to be sick and our bodies to be cursed. They have **blinded** us from seeing our Maker.

SOUL BLINDNESS

Our enemy the devil operates through our sin. Our sin empowers him to further separate us from God's Spirit. The Bible tells us that Satan, the god of this world, works to *blind the souls of men* (II Corinthians 4:4). This indicates that a person's very soul- that is his mind, his will, his emotions- can be blinded. This soul blindness is what prevents the afflicted person from seeing the glory light of Jesus Christ. It's what blocks the light of Christ from shining fully into his life. And without that light, he cannot see Jesus in his heart of hearts.

Relating physical blindness to spiritual blindness, you have a good illustration of God's revelation. You begin to understand that *your ability to see God revealed is directly related to the condition of your spirit and your soul.* Just as your physical condition affects your ability to see an object in a room, so your spiritual condition affects your ability to see your Maker, as does your proximity to Him. The "object" is right there before you. God *IS* uncovering Himself before your very eyes! He's showing Himself to the whole world, all the time! But soul blindness keeps many people from seeing Him as He really is.

This is a tragedy, but not a hopeless one.

The good news is that this soul blindness is healed when we ask God to heal it! The blindness need not be chronic; it is only permanent if we allow it to be. If you want to see God, you must ask Him to un-blind you! Ask Him to take off whatever sin blindfold is wrapped around your spirit and soul. Psalm 146:8 (NIV) says that "the Lord gives sight to the blind". That is, He makes us see what we could not see of Him before- when we ask Him to, and when we abandon our sin.

What we see or don't see in the spiritual realm is greatly up to us. What we choose to open or close our spirits to will have a sure impact on who we become in this life. It will shape our personal belief systems- our faith or our lack of faith in God. When we view something eternal in our eternal spirits, we are changed. Eternal things coming into clear focus will affect the decisions we make and the actions we take in this life. What we "see" spiritually will affect our behavior, our state of mind, our contentedness.

God shows Himself to mankind through His Word, the Bible, and through His mighty works. He shows Himself through His creation, the natural world, even in our own incredible bodies. He shows Himself to us in our day-to-day experiences, and by day and night dreams and visions. God lets us feel the blanket of His Spirit's love and comfort, which feels good. He also lets us feel His chastening and purification, His intolerance of our sin, which doesn't feel good at first, but it does after a while. God reveals Himself to us in part now (I Corinthians 13:9), but there will come a day when we will see Him fully, in all of His brightness.

GLIMPSES OF GLORY

If I told you, "I have seen God", how would you respond? Would you believe me, or would you doubt my sanity? Would you be intrigued to hear more, or would you want to change the subject? Would you be happy or frightened for me? Would you want to experience what I did? Would you be able to tell me of your own experiences seeing God?

Well, I am writing this book to tell you that I HAVE seen God. Not yet in the fullness of His glory, but I have seen glorious *glimpses* of Him, through His works all throughout my life. Real, undeniable, unexpected miracles have taken place in my life and in the lives of people I know. I've felt God's presence in dreams and visions. I've heard His Spirit clearly speaking to me, when I was listening for Him. I have felt His warm light upon my spirit, my soul, *and* my body.

I realize my claim may shock you. You could be rolling your eyes at me right now; I know that! (Though I hope you're not.) Whether or not my words seem relevant to your life, I hope you keep reading.

People talk about men in Bible times, like Adam and Moses, men who were said to have seen God. And they won't deny that was real... for them. They accept that *those guys* saw God and God saw them. But they say, "It's not that way for you and me. It doesn't work that way anymore. God can see us but we can't see Him."

I disagree.

We DO see God today. We see Him in the God-man Jesus.

The God-man Jesus. The Almighty God, incarnate. Fully God and fully man. He was and IS "God with us", Immanuel. All the fullness of the Godhead dwelt bodily in Him (Colossians 2:9).

Jesus said He would show Himself to the person who loves Him. He said, "The person who has my commands and keeps them really loves me; and whoever really loves me ...I will love him and will show Myself to him. I will let Myself be *clearly seen by him* and make Myself real to him." (John 14:21 AMP) This promise was spoken to people who loved Him when He walked in human flesh on this earth. But it was not a temporary vow made just between Him and those select followers at that time. It was a promise intended for ALL His followers, spanning across generations and over all the nations, throughout all eternity! The promise was written down so we would know it--so the whole human race would forever claim it. The Word of God will stand forever (Isaiah 40:8). So when Jesus, Who *is* God, promised to show Himself to those who love Him, He meant just that! *Every person must be willing to love Jesus if he is to see God. He must be willing to see Jesus when He shows Himself real.* Only then will His glory be unveiled- in warm, comforting acceptance and forgiveness that compares with nothing you've felt before. The specific ways that God shows Himself are different for each individual person, because each man and woman has unique needs and experiences. But His revelation comes always with several common threads of truth, love, and *light*.

I said before that the LIGHT of God must first enter the spirit of the person if he is to see God on a spiritual level. The way that light enters is through Jesus Christ, the Door (John 10:9). Jesus said, "I have come as a Light into the world, that whoever believes in Me should not abide in darkness." (John 12:46 NKJV) Every time the glory of God is revealed to men in Scripture, there is a bright *light* present. That is because "God *IS* light, and in Him there is no darkness at all." (I John 1:5 KJV)

Once God's brilliant light filters through the "lens" of your spirit, it travels through the inner filters of your soul, through all of your pre-supposed notions of Who God actually is. It continues sifting through the "rods" of your intellect and "cones" of your past experiences, being recognized for what it really is- DIVINE TRUTH! Then the Light, which is Jesus, is translated into a message you eagerly receive. It becomes an intricate image of love that is imprinted on you in a unique way. And your life is changed.

That's how it's been for me.

THE ARM OF GOD

I continually have a picture in my mind, a picture of the arm of God. I first saw it in a dream when I was 11 years old, and I have seen it several times since then, in night dreams and in daydreams. In this picture, God's arm is strong and muscular. It is reaching downward, with fingers outstretched, not in a fist. The arm is firm and broad and brightly illuminated. Bright light shines on it from above and behind, and light shines out of it. Behind it are large colorful clouds, moving and glowing. They look like star nebulae. When I look closely at it, I see the arm is *JESUS*. I see Him clearly there. The Bible speaks often of the arm of God. It refers many times to JESUS as being (at) God's powerful right hand. *JESUS* is the part of God that reached down to man, by becoming a man Himself. He is the mediator who connects God to us. See Jesus, and you will see God the Father. (John 14:6-11)

As I look even more closely at this powerful outstretched arm of the Lord, I also see *myself and my fellow Christ followers,* sealed upon it. The Lord Jesus has you and me sealed upon His arm and heart! (Song of Solomon 8:6) We are His beloved, and He is ours. Just as Christ Jesus is the extension of God to the world, those who follow after Him are the extension of *HIM* to the world. Functioning like fingers, we are connected to Him. We are useful, necessary parts, functioning together with Him to touch people on a spiritual level.

In the chapters following, I will tell you about the power I have seen, the power of God's great arm, and what His hands are to me. They are writing hands, having carefully inscribed the greatest message of all time to you and me and all the world. They are hands pierced through and arms extended on a cross of shame, to save us. They belong to the master Potter, Who made us and everything else in this fabulous universe. We can reach out to take things from God's hands, as they PROVIDE for us always. I have felt them embracing me all around, tightly engulfing me in an outrageous PURE LOVE that never ends. These hands are clean, and they have all healing power. They are mighty enough to break our chains. The Lord's arm shields us from danger; it rescues us. And we can hold these hands and rest in these arms forever, in a sinless world without end.

As I tell you about all this here in greater detail, I hope you will come to understand why I believe that Jesus is real, why I believe that He is Who the Bible says He is. I hope you hear my words with your soul and *see* them with your spirit. I hope the Lord Jesus *unveils* Himself to you as you read this book.

"I anoint your eyes with eye salve, that you may see."
-Words of Christ recorded in Revelation 3:18 (NKJV)

CHAPTER 3

HANDS SEEN BY ALL

"For since the creation of the world, God's invisible qualities- His eternal power and divine nature- have been clearly seen, being understood from what has been made, so that people are without excuse." Romans 1:20 (NIV)

The first time I actually thought really hard about God's revealing Himself to men of Earth, I was a third year undergraduate student sitting in a Bible Doctrines class at my Christian university. My professor spent some time leading me and my classmates in a discussion about the general and specific revelation of God to man. Before that day, I had never heard of "general" revelation versus "specific" revelation. I had only thought of "revelation" as the title of the last book of the Bible, and that it had a lot to do with the end of the world. That was the day I learned there is more to revelation than that. It isn't something that's only *going to* happen in the future. It's something that's *been* happening all along, and *is* happening right now.

Despite his quirky ways, "dorky" even, my Bible Doctrines

teacher had a very direct way of communicating God's truths to me. Let's call him "Mr. J".

REVELATION AND MR. J

Mr. J was a soft-spoken, timid sort of man with a balding scalp and big round, protrusive eyes- protrusive enough to be called "bulging". His eyes were lightly colored and intense, but kind. He had big teeth that seemed even bigger when he laughed, which he did often. Mr. J's fingers were stiff, as though he may have suffered from some form of arthritis. When he pointed at something, he would not close his fingers; instead, he would "point" with his whole hand stretched out. To see Mr. J on the street, you would not think him to be a highly influential person. But he *was*, to me. He spoke God's Word of truth to me in a way that was new and exciting. When he spoke of God the Father and God the Son and God the Holy Spirit, I was on the edge of my seat the whole time. Mr. J's love and appreciation for spiritual things really rubbed off on me.

On this particular day, Mr. J began teaching our class how that *all* men receive general revelation from God, by several means. He explained how God unveils Himself to every person in certain same ways, regardless of where they live or what culture they are born into- how that *all* men and women are given evidence of their Maker. This general evidence is called "general revelation" by Bible scholars. One example of this evidence is our natural environment. Everything around us. Those classic elements of earth, air, water, and fire. Every person ponders them at some point. We ask, "How did all this nature come to be? How does it function so perfectly well all the time, seemingly on its own? Why is there so much order, so much consistency and parallelism, and yet so much variance, so many intricate differences within it?" These questions bring men to seek out their Maker. The fashioned works of a divine Creator point to His character. Many men express faith in a master Designer, solely based on the design they see all around them. This is why so many people groups over the ages have worshipped- even sacrificed themselves to- the sun, the moon, the stars, trees, water, earth, mountains, even animals. They sense that no man could ever have fashioned such things. "The heavens declare the glory of God; the skies proclaim the work of His hands." (Psalm 19:1 NIV)

Another evidence we have of God's existence is our innate conscience. Conscience is inherent in our character. Men generally seek out truth and uprightness in their lives. Throughout their lives, they stop to consider internally what is right and what is wrong. Even the men and women in the most remote places of the world- such as the indigenous peoples of South America, Australia, and Africa- do this! It is not something that comes from modern education, urbanization, or organized religion. *It comes from God.* Even Adam and Eve had a conscience, in the Garden of Eden. They knew what was wrong, *before* they chose it, because *God put this knowledge in them*, just as He has done for us. When Adam and Eve first bit into the fruit, they may have remarked to one another, "We shouldn't be doing this". God had given them a built-in sense of their own obedience to Him. They were supposed to *choose* obedience. When they chose *disobedience* instead, they knew what they were doing was wrong (Genesis 3:10-11), but they did it anyway. And afterward, they *knew* they had sinned. Their conscience told them they had done something they shouldn't have done.

As the offspring of Adam and Eve, we humans as a race ask ourselves, "What is true and what is untrue? Which actions and behaviors are acceptable? Which are not acceptable, and why not?" The issues of morality and ethics tug at the souls of all men and women, regardless of their particular place in the world. The search for absolute truth, the longing for justice, and the pursuit of a clear conscience compels many hundreds of thousands of men to seek after God.

OK, so God shows Himself generally through nature and through the human conscience. But this general revelation is limited. It is misinterpreted rather easily and rather often, by men. By itself, general revelation cannot bring a person into the fullness of truth about God. It cannot bring a person into a redeeming relationship with Jesus. *It cannot save anyone from eternal damnation.* For that, they need *specific* revelation, which God also readily gives. Mr. J taught me about this, and now I'm teaching *you* about it! (Mr. J would be so proud.)

Specific revelation differs from general revelation because it is how God reveals Himself *individually* to each person. Scholars also call this "special revelation". It is "special" because it is not the same for all people. It's *custom-made* for each person. Specific revelation is God reaching out to meet a person's individual needs, showing him what he needs to see at the time he needs to see it. If God has shown you things in your life, and you *know* in your spirit that they came from Him, then you know exactly what specific revelation is, because you've received it. It is just for you, at a particular time in your life.

This special unveiling of God's work and character reaches us in many ways. It comes to us through verbal and written communication. That time you read those Bible verses and they seized hold of you somehow. Or that time you heard a person talking about Jesus, and you felt drawn to the words. Whenever God's Word is spoken or written to a person, that person has received special revelation. Special revelation also comes through signs and wonders. Miraculous experiences. God doing something impossible in a life. This could be in the form of a physical healing, an incredible close call, or a bunch of amazing "coincidences" that are just a little too coincidental to actually be coincidences. Specific revelation also comes through visions and dreams, through theophanies and angelic visitations.

Going back to my Bible Doctrines class that day, as Mr. J was explaining all of this, asking and answering questions of us students, it hit me like a ton of bricks: *A person could go his whole life and totally miss his own specific revelation from God.*

SPECIFIC REVELATION *ABOUT* SPECIFIC REVELATION

I sat there in my desk in that sunny upstairs classroom eighteen years ago, and I felt my mind being opened, like a curtain being pulled off a glass window. I was receiving specific revelation *about* specific revelation!

In my mind, I saw the people of the world as being in a huge crowd. Together but alone. I saw more tribal people than any others, the kind of people that live way out in isolation from others. As I thought about God and about this vast crowd of people, all so different but so alike too, I realized that *many of these men and women would spend their entire lifetime appreciating their Creator only through His general revelation, but never coming to know Him through His special revelation.* I imagined what it would be like to never have heard or seen the words of God, to never have seized hold of their promises of hope, to never have heard the name of Jesus. I imagined what it would be like for a person to experience healing, divine protection, miraculous provision, but not recognize those things as God's hand at work in his life. To see the work of God's hands, but never touch those hands, never hold them.

In those moments, a flood of urgency took over me. I began to weep. Right there in front of my classmates and my precious wonderful teacher, Mr. J.

Tears came fast and furious, as I felt grieved in my soul over what I was seeing, what I was *knowing.* I wanted to scream over it. I wanted to shout at my classmates and ask them, "What are we *doing* sitting here? We need to get out there and tell everyone about Jesus! We need to go give out some Bibles! God is showing Himself, and people are missing it!" I was overcome with a sense of intense responsibility, knowing full well that people are dying every day, completely blinded to the specific revelation of God in their lives. *Having missed out on the hope of heaven, on the freedom of sin's forgiveness.* I looked to Mr. J and asked him about all those people. "How will they ever see the full truth and goodness of God? How will they *know* His love?" I asked him. He looked at me with great intensity, right in my eyes, and he said, "They *won't.* Unless we show it to them." I nodded in silent agreement, tears still running down my cheeks.

That was a pivotal moment for me, because I realized my place in the whole scheme of God's plan. I realized that *I was an integral part* of how God was revealing Himself to the world in this current time. *I* was a messenger girl, equipped with simple but powerful truth that had already influenced my life for good. Just as Mr. J had given me God's message, I knew I HAD to give God's message to anyone I could. God put all those people on my mind for a reason. He was telling me to love them enough to reach them for Him, *as His outstretched finger,* to touch them with a heavenly love.

I want you to imagine something for a moment. You can't close your eyes to imagine it. (You're *reading!*) So keep reading... but *as you read*, imagine this story being played out:

Imagine a bouquet of flowers sitting on a table in a decorative room in which a party is going on. Everyone is busy talking, laughing, and dancing- but everyone in the room can smell the flower bouquet. Some are very aware of the bouquet's scent, while others only notice it faintly. There are 20 people in the room. Five of them do not see the flowers on the table at all. Fifteen of them do.

Of those fifteen that see the bouquet, ten folks notice the **types** *of flowers in it. They appreciate the individual beauty and uniqueness of each type of flower in the bouquet. Half of those folks come up to it and observe its beauty very closely. Four who know about flowers appreciate the fact that the flowers on the table are quite expensive and rare, and they are very fresh. Two of those note that there are several purple saffron blossoms in the bunch. They both admire the saffron for quite awhile, knowing that it is the "king of spices", the most precious spice in all the world. They remark about its beauty but also of its healing qualities and usefulness.[1] One man asks the party host if he may take home one of the flowers.*

Instead, the host gifts him with an entire saffron plant from his garden. The plant is alive and thriving.

The guest leaves the party to begin studying this precious plant, his new gift. He recognizes its worth. He studies diligently and develops a keen skill in isolating the bulb-like croms from the plant, in order to clone the parent plant. He continues cloning saffron plants in this manner, until he has an entire saffron garden of his own. He extracts the crimson threads from the flower stigmas. From those threads, he makes a fragrant powder which he gives away to everyone he knows.[2]

The powder is used in cooking to enrich the flavor of foods and soups. It brings special warmth to teas and other beverages. The man's friends also use the powder to prevent illnesses. They use it to make medicinal salves and ointments which combat infection and promote healing in wounds. His friends and family notice that his saffron powder makes them feel good. It makes the winter seem less dreary. It relieves their tension. The man continues to give away the spice and convinces many others to do as he has done. He teaches people whom he meets, how to extract the stigma threads and grow their own plants. He visits the party host frequently, who gives him even more plants with many more healing properties. He changes his community and, ultimately, his world.

The pretty room you imagined represents this spinning globe; the party guests are the people living on it. The bouquet is the truth of God. The party host is God the Father; His living gift is His Living Word, Jesus. The plant's offspring represent the saints of God in Christ, the partakers of His righteousness. The fragrant powder is God the Holy Spirit, converting lives, making them alive and sweet-smelling.

ALL the party guests smelled those flowers. They all knew the bouquet was there. But some never really saw it. Several guests did see the flowers, but they did little or nothing with them. Only one man realized the full potential of what the plant could do, the change it could make.

And now I ask you, Who are *you* in that room? Are you one who only delights in the fragrance of God, but you don't really know where it comes from? You come to the party and leave with nothing. Have you partaken of the rich value God the Father has given you, in His Son Jesus? How deeply? Just enough to appreciate it, or maybe to utter an "ooooo" or "aaaah"? Or enough to *give it away*? Has God given you specific revelation in your life through His Word or through some divine intervention? Have the eyes of your spirit been open to encounter Him fully, to see Him the way He intends for you to see Him?

It would be a tragedy if you only ever see God as a law giver, as a Ruler, or as a Creator - but not as your adoring eternal Father. I implore you to think about how your Father has been working your life experiences together for your good. Consider miracles He has worked for you, how He's blessed and protected you all through your life. Don't miss the healing He wants so badly to give you.

God *IS* showing Himself to you. Open your eyes to see Him! Do it intentionally, courageously, do it on faith. Seek Him daily.

You *WILL* be changed. You will *not* be sorry! You *WILL* make a difference! If your neighbor is blindfolded, you have the means to show him his Maker! After you see for yourself, then you'll help your neighbor see, just as the man at the party helped those around him.

Don't wait until you leave the party, to recognize God's specific revelation in your life. It will be too late then to do anything with it.

Recognize it *now*.

> *"The secret of the sweet, satisfying companionship of the Lord have they who revere and worship Him. He will show to them His covenant and reveal to them its deep inner meaning." Psalm 25:14 (AMP)*

CHAPTER 4

A WRITING ARM

"Suddenly the fingers of a human hand appeared and wrote on the plaster wall, near the lamp stand in the royal palace. The king watched the hand as it wrote. His face turned pale and he was so frightened that his legs became weak and his knees were knocking." Daniel 5: 5-6 (NIV)

Imagine receiving a love letter that grabs your heart so tightly, you just can't read it enough times. You read this letter over and over again, and you delight in it each time, because its very words fill you with life breath which lightens your burdens and lifts you off the ground, enabling you to defy gravity. It makes you feel good about yourself, but also makes you want to be a better person so you will please the one who loves you, the writer of the letter. In the letter, your lover tells you how you are deeply cherished and accepted exactly the way you are-- that you are treasured beyond your greatest imagination-- with an obsession that will never stop. You carry this letter around with you, keeping it close to you so you can read it whenever you want. You wear out its paper by unfolding and re-folding it so many times. You read it so much that you actually memorize it. You can't go a day without thinking of it. It becomes a part of you.

Love letters have a way of doing that-- becoming part of you. For centuries, people have used writing to communicate undying love for one another. A soldier at war writing to his family back home, a man and woman pledged to be married but geographically separated for a time, a dying woman dictating her last words to her children, a young man writing to his estranged brother, asking him to please come back, a girl reaching out to a friend in trouble. *Ink is a common medium used to express the emotion that has been called the most powerful energy in the universe: Love.*

But ink can also be used to express dark and frightening things. It's plenty fun to imagine receiving a love letter. It is *not* any fun to imagine receiving a letter communicating death, destruction, or ill will. Imagine receiving a death threat in the mail. Or a written notice that your child has died in combat. A lab report confirming the tumor is malignant. Divorce papers you don't want to sign. I've never received any of those things, but I can imagine how they would terrify me if I did. Such things also have a way of becoming a part of you.

The fact is, words have power. Power for good or evil influence in a life. Power of love or hate. Power to give hope or to shatter it. Written words can live for a very long time. They can be brought back to mind repeatedly. They can be just as meaningful over years of time, even more so, as they were the day they were written.

THE WRITTEN WORDS OF GOD

God uses words to communicate with men. He reveals His identity, intentions, and desires through words. We typically think of God *speaking* His words. The Bible is full of times when "the Lord spoke to (so-and-so)...and *SAID*..." something. It's easier for me to picture God *speaking* than writing. Maybe that's because in Scripture, He speaks aloud many more times than He writes.

But He *does* write!

About what?

Let's look at four examples:

1) THE WRITING ON MOUNT SINAI - A CALL TO RIGHTEOUSNESS

In Exodus chapter 19, God tells Moses that He is going to prove Himself to the people of Israel, *so they will listen* to Moses and forsake their sinful ways. The sky fills with thunder and lightning. A thick cloud descends on Mount Sinai. A trumpet sound is heard by all, loud enough to startle them, and they tremble. Fire burns on the mountain, covering it in smoke. The mountain quakes. The trumpet blast grows louder and louder. The Israelites are frightened of God's presence on the mountain. Seeing the intensity of the lightning, the fire, the earthquake and smoke, and hearing the thunder and the loud trumpet, the people tell Moses it's a good thing *he's* the one going up the mountain to meet with God, not them!

Moses *does* go up on the mountain. He has several meetings with God there. I want to call your attention to when God writes His commands on two tablets of stone there. The tablets were

29

prepared by Moses and *"inscribed by the finger of God."* (Exodus 31:18 NIV) "They were inscribed on both sides, front and back. The tablets were the work of God; the writing was the writing of God, engraved on the tablets." (Exodus 32:15-16 NIV) It's very clear in these verses, that the words were *not* Moses' own written words. They were *God's words.*

When Moses carried the inscribed tablets down the mountain back to the camp, the skin of his face SHINED in such a way that everyone was afraid to get near him, even his own brother, Aaron. Moses did not know at first that he was glowing light. He didn't realize the visual effect God's glory light had on him. If the people of Israel began doubting God's existence, one look at Moses' glowing face would convince them that he wasn't dreaming this stuff up. *This* is one way God used writing to reveal Himself to His people. He got their attention. Those stone tablets did not read like a love letter. More like a list of do's and don'ts. God wrote those words because He loved His people enough to warn them of the fatal effects of sin. His writing on the tablets served as a lingering visual reminder of His call to righteous living. God's delivery method was pretty effective, because we're still being reminded of that call. But people are still ignoring it.

"Stop sinning", God writes. And He lets us *choose* whether or not to obey.

2) THE WRITING ON THE BABYLONIAN WALL - A WARNING OF IMPENDING JUDGMENT

In Daniel chapter 5, we read of King Belshazzar's party. You know, the one that didn't end so well. Belshazzar, son of Nebuchadnezzar is joined by a thousand of his wealthy lords, for a great feast. Wives and concubines abound, as does the wine. The scene is riotous, with lots of drinking and hilarity going on. The king and his friends drink from gold and silver cups which Nebuchadnezzar had removed from God's temple in Jerusalem. As they take in strong wine from these sacred vessels, they praise the gods of gold, silver, brass, iron, wood, and stone. The event is interrupted by the sudden appearance of a mysterious lone hand, with fingers illuminated by the candle flame shining against the palace wall. The sight of it frightens the king greatly. It sobers him, terrifies him, even before he knows the full meaning of its message. The hand inscribes words upon the wall, words that Daniel interprets for him that very night. Words of finality and judgment, telling Belshazzar that he has dishonored and disgraced the Lord of heaven and his temple, failing to recognize the One Whose hand held his very breath (Daniel 5:23). The writing on the wall tells the king that his time is up; his reign is over, and the Babylonian kingdom will be divided. Sure enough, Belshazzar dies that night, and the "writing on the wall" becomes known by all people of the time, as accurate prophecy.

God had written His commands. Now He wrote a consequence for failure to obey those commands. The consequence was death. Again, God was communicating the fatal effects of sinful living. And He was doing it in writing.

"You'll be judged", God writes to us. We can act like we don't hear it, or we can live like we *do* hear it.

3) CHRIST'S WRITING IN THE SAND- WORDS TO GRANT PARDON

In John 8, we read of the adulterous woman. It's morning and Jesus is teaching in the temple court. A woman is brought before him, by religious leaders of the day. This woman has been caught in the act of adultery; she is guilty as charged. The penalty for her action is death by stoning. Jesus is asked to give her a sentence. The religious leaders are hoping to trap Him in a mistake, to accuse Him of wrongdoing. Jesus, ignoring them, stoops down toward the ground and writes something there with His finger. Whatever He writes causes the woman's accusers to cease their sneering and scorning. They leave the place, leave Jesus and the woman, and Jesus tells her, "Go and sin no more." She has experienced pardon for sin, delivered through writing.

31

Some people believe that Jesus wrote in the ground the same words that had appeared on the Babylonian wall. Others think He wrote the secret sins of the woman's self-important accusers. Whatever He wrote, it was enough to silence their tongues and hearts. It was enough to make them see their own shortcomings, their own imperfections. Enough to spare a sinner of certain death. His written word, the Bible, is *still* doing this. We read the Bible and see our need for redemption. We read the Bible and *receive* redemption.

"You need pardon for your own sin", God writes. And then He lets us agree or disagree with Him on that.

4) The Writing of the Names- On Record for Eternity

Jeremiah 17:13 speaks of those whose forsake the Lord, those who reject the fountain of living water. It says they will be *written in the earth.*[1] The "earth" in this verse refers to a burial ground. To be written there is to be on record as a resident there. This is alluding to eternal death. Eternal separation from God.

By contrast, Revelation 21 speaks of those whose names are written in the Lamb's book of life. It describes a place where God's glory is the light, a place where no darkness abides, no night. Where nothing unclean and nothing false will be permitted to enter. This is heaven. Eternal life. Your name is either written in the Lamb's book of life, in heaven, or it's written in the earth, as Jeremiah described. God's divine hand is keeping the record which determines your eternal destination.

"You will spend eternity with Me or away from Me; accept My pardon", He writes. *"The choice is yours."*

If *You* Were a Bible Story

If God wrote about *you*- that is, if your life were a story in the Bible- what would people learn when they read it? Seriously, just think about this for a minute. I am not suggesting that your story be added to the Bible. I am suggesting it be *compared* to the Bible!

Sometimes I think about this, for myself. I think, "What kind of Bible character would I be, if my life was recorded in Scripture? How would my experiences influence the world, for God or against God?" Whether you believe the Bible is all true or not, you have to admit it's full of some pretty spectacular stories. Stories of people and God. People loving God, disobeying God, running away from God, running toward God. Stories that make us say, "No way!" - but then we keep going back to them in our minds because they increase our faith, and some of us tell them to our kids because we want them to trust God no matter what.

One reason God gave us the Bible is so we could closely associate with the people in it. Our stories correlate with theirs. The ways that God showed Himself to people in the Bible correlate to how He shows Himself to *us* right now. Part of our special revelation is God saying, "I did this for so-and-so in Scripture; I can do it for you."

The written Word of God is a MAJOR way God has unveiled His glory to the world. Some people say they aren't convinced God's real, because they've never seen Him and they can't believe in what they can't see. They don't hear Him and they can't put trust in someone they can't hear. They can't feel Him and can't develop an attachment to someone they can't touch. Do you realize people said the same thing when Jesus walked on this earth among men? Jesus was God in the flesh; He could be seen, heard, and touched. And He showed Himself as God during His public ministry, healing people of infirmities, making blind people see, even making a dead man alive after he'd been buried for four days. And people *still* didn't believe He was God!

SEE IT TO BELIEVE IT

Thomas was a friend of Jesus who had seen Him work miracles. He saw His power and yet, when Jesus raised from the dead and returned alive, Thomas did not believe it was Him until he could see the prints of the nails in His hands and touch the hole in His side where He had been stabbed with a sword.[2] Thomas had the attitude, "I'll believe it when I see it." Many of us share that attitude with Thomas. But even when Jesus shows Himself to us, we don't see Him for Who He is, and so we don't believe He can help us through this life. Or we are convinced He hasn't shown Himself to us; so we don't believe.

Thomas's story is just *one* that is told in the Bible *for a reason*. I believe all the "stories" in the Bible were given to us so we would have many real personal examples of men and women we can relate to. People with real problems, people with the same issues that plague you and me. God showed Himself to the men and women of Scripture, and *their experiences were written down so we could relate to them and see Him through their stories-* but also so we could compare them with our own incredible stories.

If you imagine your life a Bible story, I guarantee there is someone in the Bible with a similar story, one with whom you can associate, one whose story correlates closely with yours. *That is part of how God is revealing Himself to you.*

Just after the account of Thomas touching Christ's crucifixion wounds, John writes, "Jesus did many other signs in the presence of His disciples, (signs) which are not written in this book. *But these are **written** that you may believe that Jesus is the Christ*, the Son of God, and that believing *you may have life* in His name." (John 20:30 NKJV)

CHARACTER STUDY

The longer I'm alive, the more people I find I can associate with in the Bible. As I change and grow older, my associations also change. I associate with Solomon, wanting wisdom, and with Paul, being drastically changed and wanting only Jesus, more Jesus. I associate with the adulteress described above, so very aware of my own sin and the punishment I deserve, yet experiencing GRACE daily. And with Jonah, wanting to run away from the things God has called me to do--and David, pouring my heart out to God regularly in songs and writings. I associate with Peter, walking on water but then doubting and starting to sink--and Job, suffering in this life, but all the while growing more patient and seeking to trust the Lord in spite of the pain of this life. I could go on. God shows me Himself through these "stories". As I relate them to *my* story, they become so richly meaningful.

I challenge you to pick someone- anyone- from the Bible that *you* associate with. Start a study of that person. Start by making a list of the reasons *why* you associate with that person. See where this study leads. I believe it will lead you into a greater understanding of who you are- and Who God is.

In this book, as I describe specific times and places that God has shown Himself real to me, you will notice that the Bible has been a huge part of those experiences. God's Word has been much more than a rule book to me. It has been a *love letter* to me, just like the one I described in the beginning of this chapter. It has been the difference between hope and despair in my life, time and time again. It is my overwhelming comfort and convicting force.

And so, it would be **impossible** for me to write a book about God's revelation to me and the rest of mankind, without weaving in parts of this love letter and how they have reached down to me and lifted me out of a sticky, tricky web. If you are like Thomas, a person who wants to see it to believe it, **read the Bible** and *ask God to show you something through it*, about Himself and about your own past, present, and future! He <u>will</u> show you! Because *He wrote it for you*, to show you Himself and to show you the value and purpose of your very life. To show you exactly why it is worth living, now and forever!

CHAPTER 5

A SAVING ARM

"The arm of the Lord is not too short to save." Isaiah 59:1 (NIV)

Have you ever saved someone's life? I mean like someone was going to DIE unless you did something, and so you *did* something, and then that someone *didn't* die? I've never done that. I've never even had the opportunity. But I sure have daydreamed about it plenty.

For a good part of my life, I wanted to be a doctor more than anything. I would imagine myself some great medical hero, always in a place where medical heroes were scarce. In this fantasy of mine, I was extremely well-equipped to handle any disastrous emergency with great bold courage and almost superhuman know-how and strength. I would spend all of my days in a gritty sweat as I rescued all the helpless people who needed my skilled doctor hands. When I was a little girl, I played out these scenarios in my play times. I would hear or read of missionary doctors in remote places doing brave things, and I wanted to be just like them. I wanted that life of adventure and heroism. The idea of saving anyone's life is thrilling to me. Maybe there's a reason for that. Maybe someday I'll be in that type of situation and will have a chance to live out that daydream. I honestly would welcome that chance.

When we speak of "saving lives", we are generally referring to saving a person's *physical* body, preserving his mortal humanity for a while longer. To "save a life" is really just to postpone the inevitability of death. But that is appealing because it stands in utter defiance of humankind's fragility.

When we speak of "saving souls", however, the focus shifts away from the corporeal, lunging instead toward the metaphysical, the spiritual, the supernatural. "Saving someone's soul" is not something we typically imagine ourselves doing. Because we know that's out of our realm. No amount of studying or training could ever equip us to do it.

SALVATION FROM FEAR AND HELL

I first grasped the idea of "soul salvation" when I was four years old. I had heard enough about God and Jesus to be comfortable with them on a first-name basis. I had been told they loved me. I had already sung songs about their love. I had been aware of my own shortcomings as a person. Even at four years old, I knew there were things I did that were wrong. I knew I was not perfectly good. I had not sinned a lot in my tender young age, but I had done enough bad things to know I was a sinner.

One evening when my Dad and Mom were talking to me about heaven, I began asking lots of questions. I knew heaven was where Jesus lives. I knew Satan couldn't possibly live forever in heaven where Jesus is, but I hadn't really given much thought to where Satan would be living, since he wasn't in heaven. My parents answered my questions with what the Bible says of hell. I think that night was the first time I ever understood what hell is. My parents told me just enough about hell that I became scared of it. I knew I wanted to never go there.

It is a burning lake of fire. (Revelation 20:15)

Everyone there is thirsty and in torment. (Luke 16:23-24)

And worst of all, Jesus isn't there.

That night when my mother was tucking me in for bed, I told her that I wanted to be with Jesus forever. I told her I was scared about hell and didn't want to ever go there. She said I didn't have to, because Jesus made a way for me to always be with Him. She told me how everyone in the world does wrong things, and because of that, they deserve to die and go to hell. Jesus was the only man Who never did anything wrong, so He didn't deserve to die. And He certainly didn't deserve hell. *But*, she said, He *did* die. He died so I didn't have to. This made sense to me, because everything I knew about Jesus told me that He was the kind of person Who would have done that for me. I knew I wasn't perfect, but I believed He was. I understood that He was alive still, but He was in heaven with God. I understood that I'd be with Him there, too, someday, but not because I could be a good girl and be good enough. I knew it was only because of what He did for me.

There in my little bed, wearing zipper-up onesie pajamas with footies, lying snugly under my favorite blanket, I prayed to Jesus and asked Him to let me be with Him in heaven forever. I told Him I knew I deserved hell because I did wrong things. I thanked Him for dying on the cross for me so I didn't have to go there.

Ever since that night, I have experienced joy in my salvation. When I was sad or scared or lonely, I would purposely picture Jesus in my mind, think about what it will be like to touch Him when I get to heaven--and I would immediately be comforted and feel better. Every time I'd think about Jesus as a young girl, I felt loved, not scorned. I felt accepted, not ashamed. This is still true. I have never doubted Jesus or the sureness of what He did for me. Sometimes I've had cause to doubt myself, certainly, to doubt my own faith in Him. Because I am weak. But He is *strong*!

NOT JUST A MOVIE

One afternoon in my Texas elementary school, very close to Easter weekend, we had a special assembly. It was a Christian school, small even for a private school. The leaders in the school had decided to show parts of a film to the student body, for Easter. The film was *Jesus of Nazareth*.[1] Our 4th grade classroom was the largest classroom in the school, and it had no windows at all, so it was a perfect room to gather in, to watch a movie together as a group. The room was carpeted and had brown brick walls. It was a cozy, comfortable room where we could all sit on the floor and hunker down for special assemblies on afternoons such as this one. The film was shown on a fairly large television so we could all see pretty well. I only remember one scene of the film that day. That one scene is vivid in my memory. Horrible and beautiful. Frightening, violent, mysterious. The scene where Jesus is nailed to the cross. That day was the first time I had seen the death of Jesus actually portrayed on a big color screen. I had heard about Jesus' crucifixion many times. But that day I was watching it, and it was no longer just in my imagination. When they nailed his hands and he cried out in pain, I began to cry.

I am sure that I cried very quietly, because I was a very shy little girl and because all my classmates were around me, and I was self-conscious even then. But I was crying the kind of tears that keep coming, the kind that get your face all wet and you can't stop them. I knew in my spirit that Jesus was very special, that His cruel death was special. *I knew it was for me.* I had asked Jesus to come into my heart, about 5 years earlier. But until that day, I had not SEEN Jesus revealed in this way, as the suffering, bleeding sacrifice Who endured agony of the worst kind. For *me*.

I felt undeserving. I felt so deeply sad. I felt like it wasn't fair. I felt like it should have been me.

In those moments, sitting cross-legged on the floor in a very tightly packed crowd of elementary students, Christ revealed Himself to me as my *Savior*. In a big way. I watched Him die on the big TV. And as I watched, I felt surges of devotion pulsing through me. *I wanted to kiss his bleeding hands.* I wanted to wipe the blood off his face and kiss his cheeks and forehead. I wanted to tell Him I was so very sorry. That I loved Him. That I never would forget what

He did for me. As I sat there sniffling and wiping my face with my 9-year old hands, it was as though everyone else in the room was just frozen in time, and it was just me and Jesus there in the dark brick classroom. He was pouring His love on me, embracing me with the most perfect love I had ever thought about. And I could FEEL it. It was warm. Tingling. It was big. I knew Jesus' death really happened. I knew there was nothing I could do now but thank Him and love Him. I knew it was not a mistake. It was on purpose.

As Jesus showed me His suffering, I did not look away. I did not explain it away. I did not make light or make fun. I did not see an actor with fake blood streaming down his face. It was real. I SAW CHRIST in those moments, as my Savior, and I knew I'd never be the same. Because how could I deny Someone Who did that for me? How could I just go home and forget about it, like it was any other movie?

I believe I was supposed to see that film that day. I was *supposed* to be riveted to the screen during the crucifixion scene. That was how Jesus would show me Himself, in all His bleeding humanity, to me. It was the beginning of a deep adoration for Christ my Savior, an adoration that has only grown more intense since that day. I continued to go back to those images in my mind, when I would think about Him dying on the cross. When I would hear a preacher speak about the way Jesus died, I could not contain my emotion, and would often cry. I *still* cry.

In 2004, about 20 years after seeing *Jesus of Nazareth*, I would watch *The Passion of the Christ*[2] in a crowded movie theater in Santee, California. I would experience the same intimacy there, sitting in my theater seat, unable to look away from the screen, unable to deny Christ Jesus as He was in those final moments before He died. When He was scourged, I felt like screaming to the soldiers to stop! I wanted them to know they were hurting their own Savior. Their own Creator. They didn't even know what they were doing. But *I* did. I wanted to yell at the soldiers, to beg and plead with them to quit hurting Him. I wanted to burn their filthy weapons and make them suffer for what they were doing to my sweet Jesus.

Then I realized that those soldiers were just like me… and every other person on earth who needs to see Him for Who He really is. They couldn't see Him in His perfection. They didn't *get* that He was the spotless Lamb being offered up in their place. I felt so privileged to know that. But at the same time, I felt a huge sense of duty, to show people what I had seen. To do everything I could to convince them that He really did offer Himself up in their place. I wanted to stand up in the movie theater and start asking the people sitting around me if they knew this was more than just a movie. I wanted to ask them, "Do you know that this really happened? Do you know *WHY* it happened?" I couldn't imagine people sitting there and not feeling the way I was feeling.

You see, Jesus showed Himself to me as Savior.

But I had to choose to see Him that way.
Have you?

YOUR HEART THRONE

I recently asked a close friend of mine, "How did you come to know Jesus as Savior?" She replied, "I have known He's my Savior, ever since I was a very little girl, when I would picture Him sitting in my heart."

"Sitting in your heart? Tell me about that," I said.

"Well, when I was very young, someone told me that I could ask Jesus to come into my heart, and that He would come in and stay there and that He would always be the King of my heart. In my mind, I pictured my heart just like a little room, all red with red velvet walls and a red ceiling and a red velvety floor. Inside the little room was a beautiful gold throne, very ornate and fancy, just like a King should rightly have. I saw Jesus sitting on that rich throne, right there in my red heart, and I just *knew* He was really there."

Tears welled in my eyes when my friend then began telling me things about her childhood, things I did not want to believe, but that I knew were true. Her childhood was one of neglect and abandonment. Her father left. Her mother raised her, but left her alone a lot, even in her very early years. She spent many days all alone as a young girl. She remembers caring for herself and her sister even at three and four years old. At times there would be nothing to satisfy the hunger in her stomach. She learned how to take food from garbage cans, when there was nothing else to eat. At times she became lonely and frightened. But in those times, she told me, she would see that vision of Jesus sitting on the throne in her heart. The image of Him there *consoled* her. It made her feel safe and loved. She knew Jesus was in her heart, and He would help her. He was her salvation not only from sin, but from *fear* in those times. She talked to Jesus, and I have no doubt He talked to her, too.

"Jesus will always be on the throne in my heart," she declares with certainty.

And she's right. He will.

What about you? Is Jesus sitting on *your* heart throne? Have you ever come to the place where you know, deep down, that Jesus really suffered and died, and it wasn't fair, and that it wasn't for nothing?

Think back to when you first knew that. Maybe you are knowing that for the first time right now. *See Jesus there on His cross of pain, looking lovingly upon you, telling you that you are worth it.* You are worth every drop of His blood, every painful blow to His back and face, every cut from the thorns, every lashing, the tremendous thirst, the shame, the burden. YOU are why He is there. He did it because He loves **you**! He wants to be with **you** forever! He wants you to know Him! Could it be that He tried to show you this long ago, and you wouldn't see Him as a Savior you needed, or couldn't see Him because of doubt or unbelief? Could it be that you did see Him, but you have since lost sight of Him, and so must purposely look upon Him again? *Then DO it!* See the Christ, your Savior, holding out His hand to save you.

Take His hand and be saved!

"The Lord will lay bare His holy arm in the sight of all the nations, and all the ends of the earth will see the salvation of our God." Isaiah 52:10 (NIV)

CHAPTER 6

HANDS THAT HOLD THE KEYS

"I am the Living One! I was dead, and now-
LOOK! I am alive forever and ever!
And I hold the keys of death and Hades." - Jesus
Revelation 1:18 (NIV)

"Death is a part of life." We've heard that said many times. But from the beginning, death was not *supposed* to be a part of life at all. We have gotten *used* to the idea of death because it's been "a natural part of life" since the first man and woman inhabited the earth. But God didn't destine death for them. *They brought it upon themselves.* Whereas Adam and Eve knew what it was like to live in a world free of death, you and I have not known that world. That world is one without sin, because sin *is* death. "Sin, when it is fully matured, brings forth death. The wages which sin pays is death." (James 1:15, Romans 6:23 AMP) We can *imagine* what life would be like, if death were not a part of it. But it's hard to really wrap our minds around *all* that it would be, since death is what we've known as humans all this time. The death sentence of original sin is in our blood line. It's passed down to us from all the generations who sinned before us. "When Adam sinned, sin entered the entire human race. His sin spread death throughout all the world, so that everything began to grow old and die, for all sinned." (Romans 5:12 TLB)

Maybe you don't like to think about death; I get that. Maybe this talk of sin and death makes you feel uncomfortable. If so, I ask you to just hang tight. Keep reading, because what I have to tell you is important! And by the end of all this death talk, we will actually end up somewhere good. Honestly, I could not tell you about my experiences with God without speaking of death at least a little bit. Because a few of the times when He's revealed Himself to me the most obviously, have been in times when someone I knew - or someone I loved - was dying.

To understand some things about death and life, on a scale of forever, it's helpful to think about how death was first brought to mankind. This tragic event occurred in Eden, when Eve and Adam disobeyed God. The death brought on by their disobedience is a *dual* death. It is both a **physical** death <u>and</u> a **spiritual** death. These two deaths are linked to two specific trees that were in the Garden of Eden. I think it will profit us to focus in a bit on the *origin* of this death as described in Genesis, before we contemplate its *end* as described in Revelation. And doing *that* will help us to consider how God has even used death to reveal Himself to the world.

SPIRITUAL DEATH AND THE FORBIDDEN FRUIT

The forbidden fruit in Eden grew on the tree of the knowledge of good and evil, in the middle of the garden. It was the *only* tree in all the garden that God told Adam and Eve <u>not</u> to eat from. They were not even supposed to *touch* it.[1] When they did anyway, the first death they experienced was spiritual death. They both died spiritually that day, the very moment they took the fruit into their mouths, being immediately separated from their Maker by their disobedience.

A person is spiritually dead when he is separated from God.

As Adam's offspring, *every* person is spiritually dead in their natural state. Our spirits are destined to come alive, to come to know God, to abide in His Spirit, to be loved by Him and connect intimately with Him. That longing we have not to be alone...that aching we have to be truly loved...that is the desire in us to be with Him. But because of inherited sin, our "natural man" state makes us *separate* from God, and thus spiritually dead. As Isaiah the prophet said, "Your iniquities have separated you from your God; your sins have hidden His face from you." (Isaiah 59:2 NIV) *We must be made spiritually alive.* We must experience a spiritual resurrection, an awakening as the Bible describes it. (Ephesians 2:1-5) This spiritual life is gained only by accepting Jesus as Savior. By taking on His death as the ultimate sacrifice for sin, we are granted spiritual reunion with God. No longer separated from Him spiritually, but eternally ALIVE and IN HIS PRESENCE, all because of Christ's blood! So that "when you were dead in your sins...God made you alive, with Christ! He forgave us all our sins, having canceled the charge of our legal indebtedness, which stood against us and condemned us. He has taken it away, nailing it to the cross!" (Colossians 2:13-14 NIV)

PHYSICAL DEATH, TELOMERES, AND THE LIFE FRUIT

The inescapable nature of physical death fascinates me. The fact that we can't avoid it. Even the biological *process* of physical death - the science of it- completely intrigues me. With as much as we have come to know about it over the centuries, it still remains perhaps the greatest mystery of all natural phenomena. How is it that a man's spirit and soul are separated from his body at the time of death? How does that just "happen"? You don't need a genius brain to figure out that some unseen, untouchable, higher operating system is at work here. One that started the day Eve and Adam ate the forbidden fruit.

You see, just as Adam and Eve bore the curse of *spiritual death* after partaking of the fruit of the tree of the knowledge of good and evil, their sin also brought *physical* death to them. Unlike their spiritual death, this second death did not occur immediately. It would happen over years of time. It was the result of the Lord God removing them from the Garden, forever barring their re-entry, so they could not eat from a different tree, another very special tree. The tree of life.

The tree of life, also located in the center of the garden, yielded pleasing fruit which had life-preserving effects. Although the Bible does not say that Adam and Eve ate of this fruit, it does say that they were permitted by God to eat *freely* from it (Genesis 2:15). This suggests that as long as they had access to that tree and could eat its fruit, they had a way to avert physical death.[2] Had they not sinned, they may have remained eternally alive there with God, in paradise. I believe that Adam and Eve were human beings at the time of their creation. They were not angels; they were human man and human woman. But they were given the opportunity to escape physical death for a very long time, possibly forever, *because of their access to the tree of life.*

However, when they fell, this access was revoked. God drove His children *away* from the tree of life and out of the garden. He then placed a cherubim at the east end of the garden, with "a flaming sword which turned every way, to keep and guard the way to the tree of life". (Genesis 3:24, AMP) Denied access to the tree of life meant certain *physical* death for them. This death was gradual, a process ushered in by the words of God, when He told them, "(You will) return to the ground; for out of it you were taken. For dust you are, and to dust you shall return." (Genesis 3:19 AMP)

This gradual death process is taking place in you and me, right now, at the molecular level. And there's nothing we can do to stop it. I once walked unexpectedly into some specific revelation about this very thing, in the middle of taking an exam....

It was a crisp spring morning when I entered the brick middle school building with two sharpened No.2 pencils, my photo ID, a water bottle, calculator, and the test ticket I had purchased some weeks earlier, so I could take the Washington Educator Skills Test, or "WEST-B". The WEST-B is a three-part exam which measures skills in reading, writing, and math. Anyone pursuing teacher certification in the state of Washington must pass this exam. Upon entering a small classroom that morning, I was seated alongside 20 or so fellow teachers-to-be. As I began the test, I was focused on the task at hand: passing the test. Though I had asked for His help on the test, I had no expectation of hearing from God about death and life that day. I worked through the questions in order, plugging along as I had done on so many tests before. Until I got to a certain item in the reading section.

At first glance, I knew the question would be one I would like. I was asked to read an excerpt from a science article, then answer questions about it. Below the article was a black-and-white sketch diagram of something I recognized, something I knew very well. It was an animal cell undergoing cell division, in the anaphase stage of mitosis. When I began reading the article, I realized it was about telomeres. "This is great!" I thought, "Something I already know a little bit about!"

Telomeres are like little "caps" of DNA on the ends of chromosomes. Telomeres protect the DNA that gets copied when a cell divides to make a new cell. Each time a cell divides, its DNA is replicated, all except for the small ends of its chromosomes, the telomeres. Those do not get copied. They actually get snipped shorter, in order for the replication to occur correctly. A cell's telomeres can only shorten a certain number of times before it dies. Geneticists can determine the age of a cell based on the length of its telomeres. Old cells have short telomeres; young cells have long telomeres. At birth, we humans have about 10,000 "extra" nucleotide bases at the ends of our chromosomes. But as our cells lose bases each time they replicate, the cells age. And so, *we* age. As our cell telomeres get shorter and shorter, we experience the ill effects of old age. Loss of muscle tone, bone density, eyesight. Loss of memory, ability to fight infection, and the list goes on. When our cells reach 5,000 or so nucleotide bases at the ends of their chromosomes, the death process is triggered. When the telomeres are gone in a cell, the cell dies. You could say that, in this way, cells are "programmed" to die.[3]

This all would seem very inescapable, if it were not for our built-in mechanism to stop it from happening. That's right. Our bodies actually have the ability to synthesize an enzyme molecule which *prevents* this process from happening. Here comes the part that will blow your mind.

Some cells, such as reproductive cells, produce an enzyme called "telomerase". Telomerase actually *adds* DNA length back to the telomeres during cell division, preventing aging of that cell. Telomerase stops the shortening of the telomeres at the ends of the chromosomes. It is what allows for mass production of white blood cells when the body is fighting infection. It is also what causes the abnormal cell replication in cancer cells. Cancer cells replicate over and over without dying. Their telomeres do not shorten, so these cells do not age and will not die on their own.[4] This results in an accumulation of cells that are dividing out of control, what we know as cancer.

What triggers the production of telomerase in some cells but not in others, is a mystery which biochemists and geneticists across the globe are seeking to solve. As you can imagine, they're all over this. They have seen that telomere shortening is the cause of aging. And because aging causes so many problems in a body, and ultimately leads to death, they want to prevent this telomere shortening from happening. How many of our health problems would be solved if we could just figure out how to keep DNA replication going, without shortening our telomeres, but also without our cells going crazy and over-replicating? We might live forever! Could it really be as "simple" as a little enzyme molecule? If we could make our cells produce just enough telomerase to stop our cells from aging, we wouldn't die! Look it up in the genetics journals. Scientists are winning Nobel prizes for their research in this field. They are working to make a nutritional supplement which would safely lengthen telomeres. Something the world could eat or drink, which would slow the aging process, and possibly halt it altogether. They claim to have found the fountain of youth!

But there's a major catch. Drinking from it causes cancer.

The dilemma scientists are finding in their research is that in order to trigger telomerase production in cells that don't normally produce it, they must also figure out how to STOP cells from producing it after just the right period of time, because the DNA bases must have a built-in stop method, or they will reproduce uncontrollably. To accomplish this perfect balance of production and non-production, scientists must be able to force a biochemical process to *start* AND to *stop* in the body, in trillions of specialized microscopic cells, simultaneously, on an ongoing basis. Quite the insurmountable task.

Sitting there in my little undersized desk at Gaiser Middle School that fine Saturday morning, staring at my test booklet, with test pencil still in hand, my mind was flooded with visions of Adam and Eve back in the garden of Eden, eating the life fruit, and of myself in a future paradise, and of Christ Jesus resurrecting from the dead. My mind was opened a little further to see a glimpse of the glorious greatness of God, the Maker of my cells, the Maker of chromosomes and telomeres and telomerase in all of us. I looked up from my test booklet for a moment, to pause and think, wanting to relish the moment just a little. I had just come into possession of a deeper understanding of how- *biologically*- "eternal life" might be possible. God had revealed to me a plausible scientific explanation of something my spirit had placed faith in!

Could it be that the fruit growing on the tree of life, that was readily available to Adam and Eve, provided them safely with a supply of telomere-lengthening enzyme? Could it be that in their sinless state, they were allowed to freely eat a fruit which possessed the chemical catalyst to prevent their aging and dying? But when they sinned, their curse prevented them from eating of it any longer. God made sure they could not get back into the garden to eat it. But He also made sure the curse could never be lifted by man's own efforts. He generated a code which would forever prevent its duplication. This is why our attempts at re-creating this life-giving substance in the laboratory, *still* only brings death, in the form of uncontrolled cell division. Malignant tumors, genetic mutation, metastatic overgrowth of cells and tissues.

I don't know that telomerase is really the explanation for immortality. I *am* proposing that it *could* be. I don't believe scientists will *ever* figure out how to immortalize mankind. Ironically, they will die trying. They say, "Look, everyone, how close we are to cracking this code!" as they pass into eternity, many failing to see His revealing of Himself to them through that "code", failing to recognize His untouchable power. The Creator God wants the bioengineers to bow their knees in adoration of Him - to realize that He *alone* is the Giver of eternal life, the *only* One who holds the keys of death.

THE KEYS OF DEATH AND HEAVEN

So how much does all this stuff about the Garden of Eden relate to the way God is revealing Himself to mankind right now? A lot, actually.

God knew that Adam and Eve needed a way back to Him. And He knew that *Jesus* would be the Way. They needed redemption, restoration- as all men would need now, including you and me. The sin curse had to be removed if man was to ever have fellowship with God again. God desired this. He knew they would receive a second chance at living forever *redeemed* and forgiven, through Jesus His Son. The first prophecy about Jesus the Messiah was spoken by God at the same time He cursed Satan in the garden, when He told the serpent, "He (Jesus) will bruise and tread your head underfoot!" (Genesis 3:15 AMP)

I said before that God reveals Himself to us through the person of Jesus Christ. Those who claim to know Jesus Christ will tell you that His resurrection is a really, REALLY big deal. You see, when Jesus Christ died and resurrected from the dead, He completed the biggest write-off to ever occur on Earth. He cancelled the debt of sin-wages that mankind was obligated to pay. He *overcame death* by proving that He was more powerful than it was! Then He said that all people who believe Him and trust Him with their lives would be given that *same* power. They would receive the great inheritance of His sinless glory and His resurrection; they would be granted the right to share His never-ending life with the Father. *By resurrecting from the dead, Jesus gave humanity access once again to the tree of life.* Access once again to paradise! Access to a perfect place free of death and sin, a place of unending companionship with the Father. The key of death is not the only key Jesus is holding. He also holds the keys to heaven. In Matthew 16, Peter tells Jesus, "You are the Christ, the Son of the living God." Jesus replies, "You are blessed, because my Father in heaven has revealed this to you. You did not learn this from any human being. And I will give you the keys of the Kingdom of heaven." (Matthew 16:16, 17, 19 NLT) *He would not have said that if the keys were not His to give!*

In the end of the Bible, we hear Jesus speak about "him that overcomes". He is speaking of any man who accepts the inheritance of His sinlessness. The inheritance of *His* righteousness is our deliverance from death and hell! Jesus says, "To him who overcomes, I will grant to eat of the tree of life which is in the Paradise of God. The first and the last, Who was dead, and has come to life, says this. He who overcomes will *not* be hurt by the second death." (Revelation 2:7, 8, 11 NASB) That second, spiritual death that condemns a soul to eternal separation from God- has no grip on a person who overcomes it through Jesus. You see, Jesus holds the keys to that death. He can lock the gateway to that death, and unlock heaven's gates instead, bidding us entrance through them. He alone is the One Who has swallowed up death in victory, abolishing it forever! (Isaiah 25:8) He has set apart the ones who have placed trust in Him, who've recognized Him as the spotless Lamb sacrifice. He has removed the reproach of sin that we were born into. He has conquered the death that accompanied our shame.

Revelation 3 and Isaiah 22 both tell us that *once Jesus opens the door to His Kingdom for you, no one can shut it.* And once He closes the death door, no one can open it back again! I hope that you can say He has opened the Life gate for you, and locked your death gate for good!

"I am the Door. Anyone who enters in through me will be saved (will live)!" -Jesus
John 10:7 (AMP)

CHAPTER 7

HANDS TO HOLD IN DEATH

*"Even in death the righteous seek refuge
in God." Proverbs 14:32 (NIV)*

Everyone has a life story. But everyone has a death story, too. I'm not referring to the *cause* of your death, or the point in time when it will occur. I'm referring to your feelings and attitudes going into it, your approach to it, as well as your thoughts and attitudes about your *loved ones* dying. Death changes immeasurably when God is not only *IN* the picture, but He *IS* the picture. He causes the story to be a happy "ending", an "ending" that is actually a miraculous beginning.

II Kings 9 describes the violent death of a perverse and manipulative woman, Jezebel, who denied God and despised His followers. She met her death when thrown from a high window. She hit the ground and was trampled by horses; then her flesh was devoured by dogs, to become dung on the face of the fields.[1] Absalom, the notoriously rebellious son of King David and murderous enemy to God's people, became tangled up in an oak tree and was stabbed alive as he hung there; then he was stoned and thrown into a pit and buried with rocks (II Samuel 18:9-18). King Saul, oppressed by evil spirits throughout his lifetime, ended his own life by purposely falling on his sword. His three sons did the same thing (I Samuel 31:4-6). Judas hanged himself after betraying Jesus (Matthew 27:3-8). These people lived lives of greed and self-glorification. Their death stories were filled with self pride, despair, and dark evil presence.

Contrast that with the violent death met by Stephen in Acts.[2] Stephen had been preaching the Word of Christ to a crowd of people, and certain religious leaders within that crowd grew furious at his words. They were enraged against him and seized him, yelling at the top of their voices, rushing at him and dragging him away from the city to a place where they could stone him. As this was happening, Stephen looked to heaven, and he saw the glory of God, and Jesus standing at God's right hand. God revealed Himself to Stephen in those final moments of his life. While enduring the painful blows of the rocks being hurled at his head and body, Stephen was praying, "Lord Jesus, receive my spirit. And do not hold this sin against these men." He died peacefully, in the midst of an angry, murderous mob. He died talking to His Lord, forgiving his perpetrators, and reaching upward to Jesus, ready and anxious to be united with Him at last. *What a death story!*

GODLESS DEATH VS. GOD-CENTERED DEATH

In my lifetime, I have been with a few people dying with God at the center of their lives, and some dying without much faith in Him, or none at all. The difference is *striking.* I have seen how death *without* God is an entirely different experience than death *with* Him, for the person dying and for the ones they leave behind. Death without God is empty, unsatisfying, something worse than gloomy. It's despairing and unknowing, leaving people to wonder about eternal destination. It is an unrealized purpose. Death with God, however, is peaceful, hopeful, a fulfillment of promise. Comforting, joyous, even celebratory, as focus shifts upward toward a new life far better than this earthly life could ever be.

I was particularly impressed with this difference when my father passed away in July of 2004. He is the closest person to me whom I have lost to death. My Dad knew Jesus and loved Him more than his own life. He dedicated his life to telling people about Him. My Dad never grew tired of the message of the Bible. It was the thrill of his life.

At the time of his death, Dad was lying in a hospital bed in San Antonio, Texas, where he had been transferred to await a kidney/liver transplant to remedy complications of diabetes. I was living in California at the time, but had visited my family in Texas a month earlier and had seen the condition he was in. It was shocking. I recall one of those last days I spent with my Father...

PEACE AT THE DIALYSIS CENTER

My family was all together at a beach condo on South Padre Island. We "kids" and all the grandkids could enjoy the ocean, while Mom and Dad could watch safely and comfortably from their patio balcony. At the time, Dad was going to dialysis two to three times a week. My mother had made arrangements for him to have dialysis at the center nearest the condo. She got him ready for the appointment, and I offered to drive him to the center and spend the day with him, so Mom could rest and maybe spend some time down on the sand for awhile. We knew the trip to the dialysis center and back to the condo would exhaust Dad, but it was necessary. At that time, Dad could barely sit up or stand. He could not walk at all. Blindness had taken his vision. Neuropathy had taken all sensory feeling from his feet and hands. The whole way there, Dad was in and out of sleep. Yet, I remember when he was awake, he and I talked of pleasant things, and of God. His level of contentment amazed me. It encouraged me to be content, too, in spite of witnessing- moment by moment- the debilitation of his condition.

At the center, Dad conversed jokingly with his caregivers. He was friendly, kind, and patient. He slept through much of the procedure that day, and when it was over, he was noticeably even more fatigued than he had been when we'd arrived. Before leaving the center, he said he needed to use the restroom for a moment, so I took him in and then left him alone, deciding to wait just outside the door, listening and ready to rush in if he took a fall or if he needed me. The restroom door was cracked open just enough so I could hear him well, as his voice was only a whisper from the exhaustion of the day, and I would not have been able to hear it otherwise. After a moment, I heard him begin to mutter something. I leaned in and blocked out all the surrounding noises so I could only hear his mumbled words. And I realized that he was praying. I had heard my father pray many, many times. But this sounded different. The prayer was intimate, completely loving and comfortable, just as though God was right there in the room with him. His prayer was for strength and help. Then he began *singing*. My father, barely strong enough to stand and sit, was *singing* a hymn of praise to God there in that dialysis center. I don't remember which hymn he was singing. I only remember the way his voice sounded. It was happy! It was peaceful and trusting. Beautiful, strong, confident. As though nothing was wrong in the whole world. It was as though he had prayed for God to minister to him, and his prayer was being immediately answered.

There in those moments, God spoke to me through His Spirit. He told me not to worry for my father. He told me He was right there with us, that Dad was not at all abandoned emotionally or spiritually. The God of all comfort was assuring my soul that Dad was going to be just fine (II Corinthians 1:3). I think I needed to be there outside that restroom door in that moment, to hear the sound of Dad's tender prayer and the sweetness of his song offering. Dad didn't know I was listening in, and I never told him.

The peace I felt in those moments was enough to carry me into the next few weeks leading up to Dad's passing. If I had a moment of doubt about God's goodness or was tempted to wrestle in my spirit instead of embracing peace, I would remember that time when God showed me Dad was going to be OK. It did more than comfort me. It *carried* me.

PEACE IN THE ICU

About a month later, I was at work at Scripps Mercy Hospital in San Diego, when I got the call from my Mom telling me that Dad was on life support and was not expected to live another 36 hours. I left on the first flight possible, with my husband and children, down to San Antonio. When we arrived, we went straight from the airport to the hospital to be at Dad's bedside. It was close to midnight. My entire family was there, and we encircled his bed. We touched his arms and head and face, held his hands, and began singing hymns and Scripture songs that had been dear to us for years, but in those moments became even more precious to our solemn hearts. As we sang and prayed, we knew the Lord was right with us. *We felt His presence*, His peace. It was the most startling peace I had felt in a long time, like a flood gushing over me, swallowing me up. I felt warm and tingly. I could *feel* Jesus right in the room with us, holding my Dad's hands right along with us as the last air filled his lungs. My Dad's struggle with diabetes was over. His blind eyes would see again; his weak legs would run and leap and stand in God's presence!

I was not afraid for my father. I didn't wonder what was happening. I knew this was the best thing that COULD happen to him. He was going to be with God. God held my whole family with His comforting arms in that hour.

When we left the ICU that night, we felt tired but also relieved. We felt sad for ourselves but so overjoyed for Dad. I remember walking through the hospital halls seeing other families in the ICU, some of them with no hope in their eyes. No peace. I'd been in hospital hallways like this many times before, as a nurse aide and volunteer. But now I was on a different side of things. *I* was the one enduring the loss. I remember thinking, "How would this feel if I didn't know Dad's with the Lord right now?" And I felt an intense heaviness at the thought of it. I wanted to go up to the other families, tell them I was sorry they were so weighted down. I honestly wondered how they were getting through this if they didn't have God's hands to hold. "How is it that these people aren't having a complete meltdown?" I thought to myself. I realized that some of them probably *were* having meltdowns, or would at some point soon. It struck me like lightning, how very blessed we were to be in the presence of God that night. To feel His loving hands. I was experiencing the fullness of Jesus' promise from Matthew 5:4 (KJV), "Blessed are they that mourn; for they shall be comforted."

PEACE AT THE FUNERAL

At Dad's funeral several days later, most everyone in attendance understood the peace I felt about Dad's passing. They were sad to lose my father, especially at the age of only 59, but they were rejoicing over the thought of him being with Jesus in heaven. We sang songs; we laughed. We brought to remembrance many of the things my father had done for Jesus' sake. But there were some people there who did not understand how we could be so joyous. Why weren't we angry? Why would God "take" a man who was doing so much good for the world? Why weren't we asking "why"? Why were we not wailing, moaning, lamenting?

The reason is simple. *We had peace.* Peace in death- in spite of our heavy sadness and grief. We all felt heaven's peace, like a blanket covering us, giving us incredible comfort that whole day. I thought over and over, "*How* could I get through this if not for Jesus?" Contrasted in my mind then were a few funerals I had been to where God was not mentioned or given any glory. There were bitter faces and countless tears, and much emptiness.

God showed me in that time that in this life, we really are *supposed* to be united with Him, the same way Adam and Eve were before they sinned. We were made to *commune* with God from our beginning. But because of sin on the earth, and because God cannot be in the presence of that sin, He cannot be with us here the same way He was with Adam and Eve. The death curse made that impossible for now. So we must go to Him, go where He is, where there is no sin. "Then shall the dust out of which God made man's body return to the earth as it was, and the spirit shall return to God, Who gave it." (Ecclesiastes 12:7 AMP)

That constant longing we all have, for peace and freedom of soul, will only be fully satisfied when we are with the Lord God of heaven. When a person accepts Jesus as Savior, he is granted eternal life with the Lord. Eternal life in heaven, far away from the grief of sin and the toil of this life. Whether you lose your life in sudden violent trauma as Stephen did, or gradually from disease as my Dad did, your inheritance will be the same: ETERNAL LIFE WITH CHRIST. And being led into that will make even death a sweet occasion, for you and for everyone around you who also believes this. Those who hold the hand of Jesus during death enter the "afterlife" without fear and trembling. They welcome it with expectancy, with hope and gladness, because they know what bright, rich inheritance awaits them. "Those who walk uprightly enter into peace; they find rest as they lie in death." (Isaiah 57:2 NIV)

DEATH'S GAIN

Knowing Jesus and walking with Him in this life does *not* guarantee you an easy life, nor an easy death. It does not exempt you from bearing the curse of physical death. But it does give you freedom from *fear* in death. There's no way around death for us. But there is a way around fear and hopelessness in death. The way is Christ.

"For me to live is Christ, His life in me. To die is gain, the gain of the glory of eternity." (Philippians 1:21, AMP) Paul wrote this fully knowing that his life could end any day. Like my Dad, Paul found his life's purpose in the person of Jesus. But he also found his death's purpose in Jesus. He knew that being with Jesus was a desired "end". *Not* a dreaded one!

"*My goal is to glorify Christ and to have His strength made perfect in my weakness. I understand that He is conforming me to His image, and I thank Him for all things, knowing that all things work together for good to them that love God. Thanks to His power to change my heart, I look forward to being in His presence in heaven someday and to being united with the glorified body He has prepared for me, free from sin, pain, and suffering. I hope to hear the words, 'Well done, good and faithful servant; enter into the joy of your Lord'. This will all be to His glory and praise.*"

- Ken Duffield (my Dad)
June 20, 2003

CHAPTER 8

HANDS THAT WIPE THE TEARS AWAY

*"The Lamb Who is in the midst of the throne...will guide
them to the springs of the waters of life, and God will wipe
away every tear from their eyes. And death shall be no more.
Neither shall there be anguish (sorrow and mourning) nor
grief nor pain anymore." Revelation 7:17, 21:4 (AMP)*

One of my favorite movies is *Corrina, Corrina* starring Whoopi
Goldberg, Ray Liotta, and Tina Majorino. In the story, a young
mother passes away and is survived by her husband Manny Singer
and their daughter Molly. Molly becomes severely withdrawn and
depressed after her mother's passing. She does not speak; she is
not herself- until she is befriended by a hired housekeeper named
Corrina. In the story, Molly's father Manny is a professing atheist.
Corrina, however, *does* believe God exists, and she begins telling
Molly that her mommy is with the angels in heaven. Although this
upsets Manny at first, he sees how it brings tremendous comfort
to little Molly, and she begins to come out of her depression. She
starts to talk again, smile, and laugh. At a mid-point in the film,
Manny tells Molly, "Heaven and the angels aren't real. They're just

things people make up so they won't be so sad anymore, so they'll feel better." Molly replies, "Well, what's wrong with that?" In the end of the story, Manny begins to pray to God, asking Him to reveal Himself and admitting that he needs God's help. Manny has witnessed the difference between Corrina's hope-giving attitude toward death, and his own empty one. He realizes his need for direction, peace, and fulfillment in this life. In his grieving, he finds comfort from above, for the first time.[1]

If you've experienced something like this in a time of sorrow, could it be that God is reaching down to you in those grief-laden moments, speaking to you tenderly, wanting to comfort you and give you a new hope? If you feel His touch that way, don't ignore it! *It's there for a reason.*

When I hear someone criticize a Christ follower for believing he'll be with God and the angels when he dies, I want to respond just as Molly responded to her father. I want to ask that person, "Well, what's wrong with that? It makes so many people feel better. It helps people not hurt!"

The closing scene in *Corrina, Corrina* paints a lovely scene of how one person's resolve to spread hope can be multiplied contagiously as hope in other people. The scene shows Molly sitting with her grandmother outside on the porch steps. Molly's grandfather has just passed away, leaving her grandmother a widow. Molly begins singing *This Little Light of Mine, I'm Gonna Let it Shine* (undoubtedly a song she learned in Sunday school when going to church with Corrina). Molly has taught the song to her grandmother, and coaxes her into singing it with her, there on the front steps. The peace Molly found because of the hope of heaven, spills over to her father and grandmother. It makes a positive difference.

Now, my intent for this chapter is *not* to promote a Hollywood film. But I felt the story of Manny and Molly Singer was a fitting illustration of what I *do* intend to communicate in this chapter: a message of healing even in death. The fact is, *having peace in death is one of the most powerful healing elements God gives His children.*

It's one of the ways He is unveiling Himself! Many who've chosen to receive the peace and comfort of God- when they suffer the loss of a loved one- can testify to the ways He makes Himself real to them in those dark days.

THE MORTALITY CONSCIENCE

When someone we love dies, we are made very aware of the cursed essence of the whole thing- the loss, the finality, the persistent, throbbing ache that lingers when you're separated from a person by death. And it's easy to see why death is truly a thing of judgment, a penalty. It feels all wrong. Like wrenching, bitter knots in your stomach.

God lets us know the reality of His existence, the truth of His Word, and the splendor of His Kingdom in heaven, through man's mortality. That constant pain you feel when someone you love is gone? That's there because in your spirit, you sense that it's really *not* OK that your someone is gone. You sense that it's *not* supposed to be that way. We are not *supposed* to "go"! Just as God gave us a conscience telling us our sin is wrong, He also gave us a sense that our physical death is wrong. No one needs to convince me that death is a curse. I know it, I *feel* it, in my spirit. The proof is all around me. I call this the *mortality conscience*. It's our inner awareness that death is a curse. It's never going to feel right. No one has to tell us death brings pain. We *know* it does.

The good thing about the mortality conscience is that it causes people to seek God. When a person is thinking about his own death (or staring it right in the face) he is often more likely to seek after God. He may begin considering the possibility that heaven and hell are not fictional places. He may start reading the Bible and praying for the first time in his life; he may even go to church. If a person has claimed to have faith in God for a lifetime, that faith is often deepened, broadened, when death comes into the picture. Prayers feel heavier, somehow more real and more important, when uttered on and around a death bed. There's just something about death that makes us think about eternity. That's on purpose! We're *supposed* to think about that! God "has planted eternity in men's hearts and minds, a *divinely implanted* sense of a purpose working through the ages, which nothing under the sun- but God alone- can satisfy."(Ecclesiastes 3:11 AMP) We are eternal beings. And if we're being honest, we will admit *we know that*, deep down. We all wonder at some point "what happens" to us, after physical death. This is a part of God's general revelation to us. He's calling us to be with Him for eternity.

Those of us who believe we'll be with God forever have experienced very real comfort in times of sorrow. We look forward to being reunited with family members and friends who have passed away. We look forward to the moment when Christ Jesus, the King of heaven, wipes away our tears for the last time. This will be a moment of intimacy! *When you touch someone's face to wipe away a tear, that is an __intimate__ thing!* You don't do that haphazardly to people you don't know. You do that to the one you care for- your child, your lover, your friend. The Bible's description of Jesus wiping away all the tears of humanity once and for all, bringing everyone into the eternal life they will never lose-- is the source of great hope to those who have grieved the loss of loved ones! The promise is real and brings peace to the soul in mourning.

I want to share a small part of two young boys' stories. Luke and Austin were two boys who died knowing that Jesus was calling them to be with Him for all eternity. These boys were raised in completely different homes far away from each other, and they died at different ages, several years apart. But both of them *knew* that Jesus was waiting for them with open, loving arms. Their stories are, in my opinion, evidence that God's Spirit is alive and well and quick to comfort us even in death and suffering.

LUKE

My friends Steve and Vikki lost their 9-year-old son, Luke, to leukemia a few years ago. Luke was diagnosed with acute myelogenous leukemia in October 2007, just before his 7th birthday. His journey with cancer became well known to many people in our community, especially because of Luke's hopeful attitude about it all. He and his family became a source of inspiration to hundreds who came in contact with them and who got to know Luke. Born into a family that professed a deep-rooted faith in Jesus Christ, Luke had heard about Jesus since he was an infant. His parents introduced Luke to Jesus at a very young age, so he learned early on how to talk to Jesus, and he came to love Him. Luke endured pain and many hard changes throughout his battle against leukemia. When things got really hard for him and his family, their trust in Jesus is what carried them through the bitter darkness. Luke's outlook was, "I'm glad God made me. He is very important to me. There would be no love without God. I know that Jesus died on the cross to take away my sins because He loved me so much. He has plenty more plans for me! I don't have time to worry about all the things that *could* happen. I am too busy thinking about all the happy things that *have* happened!"

At Luke's memorial service, his family told about an incident which had occurred at home, in a tender hour some time before Luke's death. When I heard them tell of it, I was touched and I thanked God for His sweet revelation! I knew He had revealed Himself to Luke and was now revealing Himself further, *through* Luke, to me and the 1800 others at that memorial service...

Luke's Mom Vikki had been in the kitchen and heard Luke singing in the next room. She peered into the room where he was, and found him sitting upright with his arms raised up above his head, his face turned toward heaven and his voice filling the room with joy and gladness. He was singing like he was in a choir, his voice not a faint whisper but one of bold, powerful confidence and of sincere adoration of the One he was singing about. The song he sang was *I Will Rise*, by Chris Tomlin.[2] The song is a claim to victory over death. A description of what will come when we are finally fully delivered from all our pain and sorrow. It speaks of rising up on eagles' wings before God, of hearing men and angel voices praising the Lamb of God, Jesus. Connecting His resurrection with our own. *"Jesus has overcome and the grave is overwhelmed."* These are not just nice words that sound catchy when set to music. They are a powerful faith statement that physical death is not the end of us. The grave couldn't hold Jesus down. And it won't hold us down either.

In those moments as he sang his victory song, Luke's thoughts were on *things above.* His soul was resting in the beauty of what it would be like when he would meet Jesus! I believe that what Vikki experienced in seeing her young son sing like that was much like what I experienced in hearing my Dad singing at the dialysis center years before. It was a confirmation from the Lord of heaven, pointing to a very glorious future for Luke, no matter when physical death would come upon him. Jesus was bringing peace already- to Luke's heart *and* to his mother's!

I don't think a single eye was dry as we all sang that song at Luke's memorial service. And every time I sing it now, God blesses me with a special assurance. I know that if little Luke could endure pain and physical suffering day after day for several years, and still face death with raised hands and a joyous heart of acceptance and gratitude, then I can do the same when my earthly life comes to an end. I know God will give me the grace to do that, just as he did for Luke. He will hand me the keys to His Kingdom, as he did for Luke. And death shall be no more.

AUSTIN

Austin was a boy stricken with muscular dystrophy. One of Jerry's Kids throughout his life, he and his family inspired many others to live vibrant, happy lives despite the injustices of this ravaging disease. Austin's physical limitations grew severe in his adolescence. He lost most of his mobility by age 13. He was not expected to live long enough to enter high school.

Austin had a gift for art and enjoyed designing sets of greeting cards every year, which could be shared with friends and family. Austin made his last set of cards around age 13. A card he sketched showed him running up to the top of a hill, where Jesus sat. His wheelchair sat empty at the bottom of the hill. In explaining his choice of design for his card, Austin said he was looking forward to going to heaven, where he wouldn't need his wheelchair and where he could sit on Jesus' lap and talk to Him.

Austin loved football and wanted to defy his odds and make it to high school so he could be part of a football team. Sure enough, contrary to even the most optimistic of his medical prognoses, Austin entered Judson High School as a freshman in the fall of 2008. The Judson High School Rockets were a notoriously successful football team, and Austin was able to get acquainted with the team and the coaches those first weeks of school. On homecoming night, October 10, 2008, Austin was wheeled out to the field to be made an honorary member of the Judson Rockets. He was 6'3 and weighed 55 pounds.

At half time that Friday night, the team awarded Austin a football signed by all the team members. Wearing a very special team jersey, Austin received his award right there on the field. As officials, coaches, and players faced the crowded stands- circled around Austin- he knew it was his chance to share the message of Jesus with the team, their families, and all the people in the football stadium that night. So he did just that. He told them what Jesus had done for him, and how much Jesus loved him and all of them. They listened and marveled at his attitude of courage and faithful perseverance. It was obvious that Jesus was the source of his great peace in the midst of so much heartache. It was obvious that he had an important message of love and truth to share with all those people.

That night, after having the time of his life there on the football field, Austin passed away in his sleep. He was 14 years old.

Austin's memorial was packed out. Many people had supported Austin and his family over the years, and they were blessed knowing him. The football team attended the memorial, and several of the team members spoke. They shared with the crowd how they knew Austin cared for them. People testified that Austin's heart was all about Jesus. That he had looked forward to being with Jesus, and now he was. I don't suppose there were many people complaining about those sentiments that day. It was good to think of Austin now with the Lord Jesus. It was right to imagine him out of his wheelchair, running up that hill to sit on Jesus' lap. The peace of God was an undeniable force at that memorial service. Jesus was speaking to the people who knew Austin, saying, "I'm real and I'm right here with you! Come to me as Austin has!" Though Austin's death was difficult to accept, *the hope of heaven made it bearable.*

If you were to meet Austin's mother or Luke's mother, you would hear more about sweet revelation. These moms could tell you stories of special revelation that would increase your faith and make you ponder the "big picture" of life on this earth and the life to come. Does death in Christ have a way of increasing the faith of those left behind? *YES,* it really does!

You and I will both face death one day. We can face it kicking and screaming, being angry with God, sorry for ourselves, lonely and troubled and full of fear of the unknown. *OR* we can face it as Luke and Austin and so many others have, with an eager expectation of shining glory and never-ending freedom like we could never experience here on Earth. The peace of God, when imparted to us in this way, is supernatural. It transcends human understanding! Those who have never had it marvel at it in wonder. Because it's nothing short of miraculous.

*"The body that is resurrected (in Jesus) is imperishable,
immune to decay, immortal. The dead in Christ will be raised
imperishable...changed...transformed. This mortal part of us,
this nature that is capable of dying, must put on immortality.
And when this perishable puts on the imperishable and this that
was capable of dying puts on freedom from death, then shall be
fulfilled the Scripture that says, 'O death, where is your victory?
O death, where is your sting?' Thanks be to God, Who gives us the
victory, making us conquerors through our Lord Jesus Christ!"
I Corinthians 15:42, 52-55, 57 (AMP)*

CHAPTER 9

HANDS I HATED

*"Then God said, 'Let us make man in Our
image, according to Our likeness'.
Then God saw everything that He had made,
and indeed it was very good."*
Genesis 1:26, 31 (NKJV)

I've been told I am beautiful by only two men in my lifetime. One was the man who married me. The other was a random guy on a Harley Davidson.

I was stopped at a traffic light, waiting to make a left turn in a very busy intersection. It was summer time in Vancouver, Washington, and the day was gloriously warm and intensely sunny. NOT a typical combination for the majority of days in the Pacific Northwest. I had taken full advantage of the spectacular radiance of the day, by taking my two kids to Cottonwood Beach to swim and play in the Columbia River and to soak up some sunrays. Now we were heading home. My skin had been kissed by the sun that day. I had just driven nearly 20 miles with the windows rolled down, adding a windblown quality to my already sandy, unbrushed hair. I was not particularly attentive to my appearance for the ride home that afternoon; it's safe to say that I was even negligent toward it. But I was so happy- so content- from having enjoyed the treasure of the outdoors in such a way that afternoon.

While sitting at the red-arrow light, a glimmering bright red motorbike pulled up next to my car, and I could not help but stare. This was the kind of motorcycle one would call a "sweet ride". The kind that compels you to look at it. As I sat gawking at the lovely creation of shiny aluminum and steel, I smiled at its lucky rider and said out my window, "That's a beautiful bike". He smiled back and nodded in affirmation, and then replied, "*YOU're* beautiful." I think I rolled my eyes as I shook my head in denial and disbelief, then looked away for a moment, completely shocked that this strange man would be saying such a thing to me. (Remember, until this point, I had only heard those words from my own husband.) My first thought response was, "This guy is making FUN of me! How DARE he?" I began to feel rather offended, and looking back at him as his red light was now turning green, the mysterious rider said to me in the most sincere and affirming tone of voice, "You really ARE." And then he nodded as if to confirm it, and smiled, and drove away.

I don't know if angels in disguise ever ride scarlet red Harleys. But that was a moment in time I will never forget.

Even if he *wasn't* an angel, even if he was an ex-hippie weirdo who was internally mocking me and keeping it to himself, he still made my entire day. In fact, those two words, coming from a random stranger, rocked my world for a better part of that week, as I felt more valuable as a woman than I had felt in a long time.

"YOU'RE BEAUTIFUL."

Why would two words, coming from a man I didn't even know, give me such a sense of belonging and adequacy, as a female fishy swimming in a vast sea of other female fishies? Why would those two words cause me to walk a little more confidently, think a little more positively, for days after I heard them?

The answer lies in a lifelong history of deep-rooted self hatred, the most powerful spiritual stronghold *ever* to take root in my soul.

You see, I remember feeling anything BUT "beautiful" as far back as kindergarten.

JAUNTY HAIR

I still remember that advertisement for that special shampoo. The ad I saw at five years old, first in a magazine and then on television. The woman in the ad had shining, bouncy curls and they were absolutely perfect. She would lift her hair up and then let it back down, and everything was in slow motion of course, as her wavy chestnut locks would fall ever-so-perfectly on her feminine shoulders, and she would toss them side-to-side while smiling confidently. Comparing that image to my own hair, I realized mine was about as non-shining, non-bouncy, and non-vivacious as a girl's hair could ever be. It was dreadfully blah in my opinion. And so I begged my mother to buy me that Jaunty shampoo, because I just *knew* it would make my hair better than it was, in just one washing. I was positively convinced that I might actually have a chance at looking like the beauty in that commercial. When I *did* finally try it and it came nowhere near fulfillment of my expectations, I was sorely disappointed, like a kid who just found out there is no Santa Claus. That was the same year an older girl told me, very matter-of-factly, that I needed to "suck in my tummy" because it was "sticking out too much". On my 6th birthday, I remember being so self-conscious about having my picture taken, that I tried to hold my tummy in while "smiling pretty for the camera".

Those are my earliest memories of feeling like the ugliest girl on earth.

This madness continued to grow inside my little girl mind. It festered and oozed like an abscess of ruin, all through my elementary years. At times, thoughtless people would compare me with some other young girl, or nonchalantly point out a flaw in my physical appearance, having no clue at all about the darkness taking root inside me. And their words would paralyze me spiritually. My grandmother would comment on the attractiveness of my older girl cousins, and in the same breath tell me not to put any butter on my bread roll. My grandpa liked to tease me when he'd first see me on my yearly visit, saying "I see you're still not going hungry". Which wasn't even true, because I was on a perpetual diet. This made me resent his words even more. Even though he was only kidding, I was not laughing. Grandpa didn't know how many times I had to eat lettuce and cottage cheese and tuna fish in my school lunch, while the other kids were eating pizza and chips and PB & J's.

I would cry getting ready to go to big events. I cried in the hotel room getting ready for Disneyland at 10 years old. Because I felt so uncomfortable in the pants I was wearing. They were tight because my tummy was STILL sticking out too much, and no matter *what* I did, it stayed that way. I was afraid I'd be riding the flying Dumbo and my pants would rip and I'd be humiliated in front of Cinderella and Minnie Mouse and every other soul in the park. Who wants to be the laughingstock in front of Goofy and Dopey? I wanted to skip the happiest place on earth and just hide from everyone instead.

THE SEEDS OF SELF-HATRED

What I didn't fully understand then, but do *now*, is that someone very evil was out to get me. The same father of lies who deceived Eve, in the Garden of Eden, was now deceiving *me*. Telling me I was hideous, that I was a joke, a big misfit. That God somehow messed up by giving me the wrong nose and the wrong hair, the wrong body and wrong talents and even the wrong personality. Even worse, this liar told me that God in His cruelty did this to me on purpose, and that He wasn't really a good God like I had thought He was. As my soul gave enough attention to those hissing lies, it was laying down a little soil for a seed to nestle into. As I gave place to thoughts of myself as a monstrous beast at 8, 9, 10, 11 years old, I watered and nourished that young seed. It began to bud into a sharp, spiny thorn that for years would jab me in my mind, will, and emotions, causing me to doubt that I was worthy of love from anyone, even from Jesus.

One afternoon when I was 11, after trying on a shirt my mother had ordered for me from a catalog, a shirt I wanted but that – of course- did not fit me well the way it fit the girl modeling it in the catalog, I started a page in my diary, "Things I Hate About Myself" and then proceeded to write a list of all the things I hated about myself. The list was long. And it was really true. I hated my whole self. That scaly serpentine enemy of mine was succeeding in his plight, and the embryogenesis of self-hatred was fully activated. The thorns kicked into full bloom.

I believe my slithery stalker had been with me all those previous times when I felt so bad about myself. I believe he saw my furious diary scribblings that day, and they gave him a steady foothold he could firmly stand on. *Because that day I allowed my heart's cry to turn from, "I'm not pretty" to "I hate who I am".* It became not only about what I looked like, but even how I sounded when I talked, the patterns of my thinking, my "dorkiness", the things I wasn't good at, like sports, crafts and cosmetics- and like getting attention from any boy. Through my high school years, I continued in this way. I hated myself so much that I wanted to hurt myself. I would do crazy things when grooming, like pull my hair – HARD-when I was brushing it. To bring pain to the scalp that produced the hair I so vehemently despised. I would slap my own face as though to punish it for being what it was. I would pound my fist against the mirror, wanting to break it so I could escape its reflection. I would regularly cry myself to sleep, wanting desperately to avoid waking up in the morning to get ready for school. Because that would mean the mirror again, and I just didn't have it in me to face it.

THE BLOSSOMING OF SELF-HATRED

As I climbed the treacherous, rocky terrain of adolescence, the thorn grew bigger. It began sprouting other thorns, prickly outgrowths pointed at others. I cultivated an inner enmity with "pretty" girls; I found it hard to be their true friend as my animus against them became profound. I tried to escape it and hide it, but those girls seemed to be everywhere, everywhere I went, making my self-consciousness impossible to ignore. My own sister, five years younger than me, had everything I didn't have in the "looks" department, and I couldn't get past the injustice of that. So my relationship with her became riddled with jealousy and covetousness, even hatred at points. I would say unkind things and think unkind thoughts, about girls just because they weren't ugly like I was. And I felt anger toward boys, too. Because it was obvious they were only giving time of day to the girls with the Jaunty hair. I could hate the girls for being pretty, AND I could hate the boys for wanting to be with the pretty girls. I could just hate everybody.

And there I was, giving PLENTY more soul soil to the thorn, which now had grown up into a life-choking weed. I was nourishing the very thing that was destroying me. Just by continuing to believe the lie that I was ugly and therefore worthless.

At age 17 I entered a Biology pre-med program as a freshman in college. This new experience came as a package deal, of course, with three female roommates. And several dormitories, and societies, and classes and hallways and a dining common- all FILLED with amazing good-looking girls my age or a few years older. And of course, there were plenty of amazing boys everywhere, too. Boys like I hadn't met ever before. It was a bit intimidating in some ways, but mostly it was exciting. I loved the academic challenges that first year brought me. I began "coming into my own" as a seriously devout student. I had always enjoyed school, apart from the social challenges, and this was as much school as I could handle, every day all the time. When I wasn't in class or working, I was studying in my room or in the library. I think I was addicted to learning, truly. Learning science. Learning music. Learning Bible. Learning art. Learning how to express myself in the big world. I was not highly involved in the social scenes around campus, but that was by choice and I was OK with it that first year. I avoided the bookstore, the commons, the recreational areas set aside for dating and hanging out. I became entirely absorbed in my studies and in my goals for the future. It was a welcome change from my high school back home. New people to meet from all over the world. Tons of spiritual inspiration. I was content and, for a time, very distracted from obsessing about my appearance. I began to focus my identity on my worth as a student, on my ability to succeed in my classes and make good grades. Until...

...that night in the girls' locker room.

SOUL ENCOUNTER IN THE LOCKER ROOM

I worked in the school dining common, with many girls and guys. One particular girl I worked with was your quintessential Southern belle. She reminded me of a Disney princess. She had that princess look, a self-important royal way about her. I'm not sure I ever saw her feet touch the ground when she walked. She just kind of flitted through air, in a flirtatious manner, always surrounded by more boys than girls, smiling a little too big and laughing a little too loud, while batting her perfectly curled-up eyelashes. This would all be fine if she was a humble, kind girl.

But she wasn't. She was the kind of girl who drew attention to herself in both subtle and forward ways. She was keenly skilled at appearing sweet and innocent, so as to charm some unsuspecting person, until some venomous strike would come from her tongue, and its victim would not see it coming. I saw right through this girl, but still she intimidated me. So I tried to avoid her at work as much as I could. I was nice to her, but felt a certain disgust when in her presence.

One evening, after a usual tiring and non-glamorous shift preparing salad croutons, filling ketchup bottles, cutting cakes, and wiping tables, I was in the locker room changing out of my uniform to head back to my comfort zone in the science building, to begin my nightly study routine. Southern belle princess girl was in the locker room, too, along with several other girls we worked with. They were talking specifically about their boyfriends and generally about boys around campus. I was listening but not taking part in the discussion. Fight-or-flight syndrome kicked in, as I hurried to finish changing so I could get out of there, and quick. But Southern belle decided to include me in their conversation, whether I wanted to be in it or not. She began asking me questions, questions to which the answers were frankly none of her business. In her pretentious and persistent way, she probed me with questions about my experiences with boys. Rather than stand up to her and hightail it out of the room, I gave in to her interrogation scheme. Within a few moments, I felt cornered by her and those other girls. I felt trapped and mocked, as they marveled over the fact that I had never had a boyfriend, never had a date, nor a kiss nor a love note- not even a hand-hold, much less anything else that they obviously had experienced in the wonderful, mysterious play land of boys and sex.

The princess reared her pretty head and began teasing me just a little, as she proceeded to make a big deal about the fact that I was so under-experienced, so virginal, so utterly boyfriendless. Then she made a comment that I'll never forget. Looking on me with pity and disapproval, she said, "Well, *honestly*, Davida- I'm not surprised at all." And then she laughed. Her manner was condescending; it exalted her obvious superiority over me. Even though I was taller than she was, I felt her staring *downward* at me. I didn't know what to say in response. The other girls didn't come to my rescue. They just stood there grinning like a pack of wolves following their vicious leader.

I don't remember anything else about that encounter; I cannot recall anything that happened after I heard those words. It may sound silly, but I think I was traumatized in those moments. ALL the feelings of inadequacy came back in those few minutes there in the locker room. All the inferiority I had ever felt growing up came exploding up through my insides, like a volcano erupting without warning. I am sure I maintained a solid and positive composure that night, because I had so much to do and I was in survival mode. But several hours later, just before calling it a day, I was in the shower quietly crying my eyes out over what had happened.

This began period of complete depression like I had never experienced. Everything became hard for me. I was in a quicksand pit, struggling to get out but slowly suffocating as my self-hatred came back full swing and consumed me. I would see that girl around school and wanted to tell her how deeply she had wounded me. I could have asked her, "Can't you see I'm still bleeding, to death?" But she was too self-absorbed to even notice my vital signs were barely detectable.

My Enemy's Stranglehold

In those few weeks, I felt so alone and socially rejected that I couldn't hold my head up. I don't remember smiling at all. I don't remember much of anything from that time, except that the days blurred together and I cried a lot. I began giving in to thoughts I had entertained back in high school, thoughts of suicide. I didn't want to live anymore because I didn't want to feel the pain anymore. I couldn't see the point of anything in my life. I couldn't see the value of my future. I couldn't see past myself and my own misery. I felt I would always be ugly and so would never be successful, never have a boyfriend, and certainly never marry. What man in his right mind would ever fall in love with ME? And it wasn't fair. I felt horribly slighted. I was angry at God and everyone else. I needed help but was too ashamed to talk to anyone about these feelings.

The devil had me in a stranglehold. And I couldn't even eek out the words, "get off me", because I had nothing left to even speak against him. At that point, he was winning.

CHAPTER 10

THE HANDS THAT MADE ME

"You have laid Your hand upon me. You formed my inward parts. Your eyes saw my unformed substance, and in Your book all the days of my life were written, before ever they took shape. How precious it is, Lord, to realize that You are thinking about me constantly!" Psalm 139[1]

Hopelessness is a dark place that no one should have to visit. I lived there only a short time; some people abide in that hopelessness much longer than I did. Not getting help is a tactic of the devil, a way he can keep you from getting out of his despair pit. Ultimately, it will lead to your final demise- a bitter, lonely, desperate kind of destruction.

I could not tell anyone what I was going through. It would only compound my feelings of inadequacy, proving my inability to handle the situation, thus proving my complete weakness and failure as a person. But I kept feeling a weighty tug to tell God everything. I mean, to tell Him *everything*. To tell Him I was really upset that He had made me. To tell Him I hated what He made, and I desired death.

SOUL ENCOUNTER IN THE PRAYER ROOM

My dormitory had a prayer room. This was a special room that was designated just for private time when someone needs to be alone with God. The room had a "do not disturb" sign, and everyone respected what that room was for, and knew not to knock when the sign was up. It was literally the only place on that campus where I knew I could go and be uninterrupted. I had never gone in there, but decided to do it one day, to really tell God exactly what I thought about Him, as my Maker. I grabbed my Bible and checked the room to make sure it was empty. Sure enough, it was available. I entered the room almost ceremoniously, knowing it was time to finally hash this out, and knowing it wasn't going to be an enjoyable process. I knew I needed to talk to God, but I really didn't know how I would muster the wit to tell Him what I really wanted to tell Him: *that He had messed up when He made me.*

As soon as I closed the door behind me, I began weeping uncontrollably. I tried to be quiet so no one would hear me. It's difficult to be quiet when you're crying as hard as I was. I lied on the floor and told God everything. *EVERYTHING.* I didn't curse Him. But I did lash out at Him, in my pain and in my anger. I told God that He was unjust and that there was nothing He could do to make this better.

It was probably an hour before I calmed down enough to do anything besides sob. Fortunately the room was well stocked with tissue boxes. I probably used half a box before I sat up and knew it was time to hear back from God. I had read my Bible enough to know that if I read it long enough, I'd probably find something to put a band-aid on the situation. I needed more than a band-aid, though. I needed direct pressure on this wound, and a full gauze dressing, and an ACE bandage wrap and an antibiotic. I had a soul wound that needed healing.

I read my Bible for a little while, still producing tears, but purposely searching for an answer from Him or even just an ounce of comfort for my weary heart. I went to the Psalms, and wandered through a few random passages, one being Psalm 139, where David the psalm-writer was talking about how well God knew him, and how He always would be with him. I read these words there: "You created my inmost being. You knit me together in my mother's womb. I praise you because I am fearfully and wonderfully made. Your works are wonderful, I know that full well."[2]

I **know** it wasn't an accident that I read those particular words.

I stopped reading and said out loud, "This is probably the only part of the Bible I don't believe is true."

Yes, I believed God had made me. I had studied enough biology to solidify my belief that I didn't just get here by random chance. I believed God had fashioned me in my mother's womb. I thought about my mother and how much she loved me, and how she's the one that told me about God in the first place. I knew she'd be torn up to find out how much I hated myself. But the part about "wonderfully made" and praising God for making me? I wasn't feeling it. I started thinking about God, and how I pictured Him to be. I imagined Him making me, fashioning me, like it said in the verse. And those images of *Jesus* came back to me, the images of Him on the cross bleeding for me. The images of Him helping all the sick people and speaking into the lives of the disciples and everyone else He ever knew. I saw His loving face, *the compassion behind His eyes.* There in the prayer room, I purposely focused on Jesus for a moment, and I had an awake dream, like a daydream, of Him looking down at me sitting there on the floor with my Bible open. It was like I could see myself in the room, but I also could see *Him* there looking in on me from above my little place on that floor.

I saw a bright beam of light shining right where I was, like a spotlight illuminating a section of a totally dark theater stage. I saw the hand of Christ extended to me, and I saw its piercing from the nail. I couldn't deny Him. I knew He was saying, "I am here and I understand."

I knew Jesus did not see me the way I had chosen to see myself. I started sobbing again, and then turned to the New Testament, because that's where I always would read about Jesus. I had a bookmark in James, so I started reading James 1. "Understand that the trial and proving of your faith bring out endurance and steadfastness and patience. Let endurance and steadfastness and patience have full play and do a thorough work, *so that you may be perfectly and fully developed, with no defects, lacking nothing.*"[3]

Those words jumped out at me, screamed at me.

"With *no defects*. Lacking nothing."

I suddenly KNEW in that instant that Jesus wanted me to stop wanting what every other girl seemed to have. He was telling me that I was **whole** just with Him. I didn't need a slim figure and flowing blonde hair. I didn't need some other more outgoing dynamic personality to be complete. I had the overwhelming sense that *I had to want Jesus more than physical beauty* and attractiveness as the world defines it. *I had to want Jesus more than I wanted a boyfriend or husband.* "Lacking nothing" meant desiring nothing. Wanting for nothing. God had allowed me to endure this trial so that I would be aware of my completeness in Jesus, and how much He loved me just the way I was. And I was reminded to be patient with the way things were going in my life. "Let patience have its thorough work." Then I thought of that girl who had made me feel so bad about myself. I felt differently toward her in that moment. Instead of feeling spite toward her, I felt sadness. *Love* even. I knew Jesus wanted me to forgive her, all the way. So I did. As I did that, I felt a **warmth** on me like a blanket. I felt relieved and so very loved. I felt like I was doing what God wanted me to do. Like I was pleasing Jesus. I stopped crying. I think I even smiled. *I felt strength in my physical body and in my mind.*

Then I gave my future to Jesus. I knew I couldn't do the rest of my life without Him. I imagined myself without a husband, and for the first time that picture didn't make me immensely sorry for myself. It was OK. I had Jesus. I told Him if He wanted me to be single forever, I accepted that. It was the first time I said that and really meant it, from the depths of my self. I knew I didn't need the attention of any man to make me complete. Jesus would do that. My prayer that had been driven by anger just two hours earlier, transformed into one of thankfulness and adoration. I didn't feel alone anymore. I didn't even feel ugly; my physical appearance wasn't even on my mind. I thanked God for showing me those Scriptures in Psalm 139 and James 1. I knew He had given them to me.

I stepped out of that little prayer room knowing that I had encountered Jesus Christ in a real way. I still felt warm. And incredibly strong! He truly filled me with a **security** that I couldn't have achieved on my own. That continued into the next months. Everything changed for the better. I had been renewed!

I didn't tell anyone about that afternoon in the prayer room.

But people started noticing differences in me. I was confident, content, peaceful. I was fun again. I began making better choices about foods I would eat. I slept better at night. I took better care of myself. I exercised and lost some weight in the coming months. I began to heal on the outside because healing had taken place on the inside. I lived for others instead of hiding from them. My whole outlook was transformed because Jesus showed His loving light to me, in my time of darkness.

NOTHING TO HATE

Five months after my encounter with Jesus in the prayer room, I was in Alaska at a singles game night in a Baptist church. I met a guy named Mark. Still completely content in my singlehood, still clinging to the truth of James 1:4 and wanting nothing but Jesus, I wasn't looking for attention or love from any guy. But God chose to bring it to me. And it was worth the wait. I had fallen completely in love with Jesus; and now He was bringing me into a new love, one that would become a picture of His love for me. Mark and I began spending a lot of time together.

One day Mark came to my workplace to take me out for lunch. Afterward, he gave me a paper on which he had written a list, titled "The Things I Like About Davida". He had written down everything he liked about me. The last thing on the list was "basically everything". Then he titled a second list "The Things I Don't Like About Davida" and below the title he had written, "I can't think of any." Seeing that list made me recall the list I had made 8 years earlier, in my bedroom, the very opposite kind of list. There were things on Mark's list that I had also written down, like my smile and the way my voice sounded. While I had hated everything about myself back then as a pre-teen, Mark's words were now confirmation of what God had told me: there was nothing to hate.

I felt like God proved Himself to me when Mark gave me that list. No one but God and the devil and me knew about that list I had written as a young girl. I felt like God was confirming what

He told me in the dormitory prayer room months earlier, that I was wonderfully knit together in my mother's womb, and that I was complete in Him.

Then about two years later, I was on a beach with Mark in Veracruz, Mexico, this time as his wife, and God spoke to me again through him. We were walking along the beach, enjoying the sand and the surf. Mark told me he had something to give me, and pulled a seashell from behind his back. He put the shell in my hand, and told me to keep it as a reminder.

"Reminder of what?" I asked.

"Keep it as a reminder of your *true beauty*," he said.

Mark began to speak into my life, running his fingers along the bumpy outside of that shell. He noted how it was rigid and had some pock-marks in its exterior. It had been tossed around in the sea for a time, and so was chipped here and there. Its outer color was not consistent throughout. Then he turned the shell over, and asked me to feel the interior of the shell. It was smooth and much softer than the outside. It was a pinkish, creamy color, much lighter than its outside. It had a hint of iridescence to it as we saw it held up to the sunlight. Mark told me that I needed to see myself like that shell. Not as something disgusting or displeasing to the eye, but something God made to show His own splendor. Something that may be imperfect at first glance, but something transforming into real beauty, beauty within. I thought of abalone shells, how they sometimes look on the outside compared to their inside. I'll always remember that day on the beach. It was *more* than a romantic newlywed moment. It was a message from God, delivered to me by my sweet groom. I still have that shell. It lives in my make-up bag, so I can see it every day when facing the mirror. And so I can be reminded that even that shell had beautiful purpose, and so do I.

True Beauty

Hate is a strong word. Whether you hate yourself or someone else, hate is evil and it's a relentless destroyer. Self-hatred births many things: resentment toward God, compulsive and self-destructive behaviors, anger and rage, social withdrawal, substance addiction, sexual promiscuity, and suicidal thoughts. I experienced almost all of these destructive results before my 20th birthday, and I am convinced that had I not seen the glory of Christ in that room that day, I probably would have gone on to experience ALL of them. Ultimately, I might have ended my own life. This stronghold of self-hatred is one that I must continually pull down. And I DO, in the name of Jesus! It is only with Jesus' power that I have learned how to walk in victory over this. I have been freed of it. Of course, my enemy still works to bind me again with it. He tempts me constantly, to return to that crippling mindset. But I come against him with the Word of Truth, and I taste victory!

Thanks to God and the Bible, I have learned how to discern between the world's vainglory, which fades and vanishes away, and eternity's **true** Glory, which will only intensify in beauty and will last forever. I know God is real because He has shown me many times in my adult life that my incorruptible beauty lies in my character and in my becoming like the person of Jesus. He has proven to me that *my worth as a person is not connected to my outer appearance.*

The world disagrees with Christ on this subject. The world shows favoritism based on outer appearances; Christ doesn't do this (Acts 10:34). The world rejects people for having physical "flaws"; Christ accepts them with all their imperfections (Romans 15:7). The world sees you for what you are on the outside, but God sees your heart (I Samuel 16:7). When I feel unfriended, unfavored, unaccepted, and misjudged by the world because of how I look, I cling to these Bible verses, and they comfort me.

I Peter 3:3-4 tells me that my soul is where true beauty lies, not in any hairstyle or jewelry or fine clothing. My heart is my true adornment. Solomon, who is known for his God-given wisdom, but also for all his wives and girlfriends, also had some things to say about true beauty. And if anyone knew a thing or two about physical attractiveness, it would be him. I'm sure the women he knew were considered "beautiful" even by today's standards. Yet, he said quite adamantly that charm is deceptive and outer beauty is fleeting, but a girl who fears the Lord will be praised (Proverbs 31:30). Solomon also said that noble character is worth far more than rubies (Proverbs 31:10). He must have known about rubies, too, since he probably owned a few, maybe many. He was known for his great wealth, yet he esteemed Godly character above his precious jewels. Solomon had all the world can offer, yet he spoke often of vanity. He recognized how superficial and meaningless earthly wealth really was. He saw what was truly valuable, and urged us to see it also.

I have seen the truths as told by Solomon, illuminated in my own life many times. I notice that people don't remember what I wear or how I do my hair. Years from now, they won't talk about how good or bad my make-up looked today, or how trendy my shoes always look with my outfits. All that is pointless vanity. What people WILL remember are my words, my attitude. They will talk about my ACTIONS. My kindness. My service, my encouragement. My art, my music. The older I get and the longer I know Jesus, the more I see His beauty shining through me, from the inside out, and THAT is what is attractive to others- ESPECIALLY anyone who has never come to know Jesus, never had an encounter with Him. In me they will see Christ's compassionate eyes. Through me they will hear Christ's loving voice and patient tongue. They will hold Christ's gentle hands. My life has been changed by the knowledge that I am a valued part of *Christ's* body. That the things I do with my time MATTER to God. These things are bringing TRUE beauty to my life. *The more I see of the beauty of Jesus, the more beautiful I am becoming.* Not on the outside, but in my *SOUL*. I feel it. I testify to it. I want YOU to experience it, too!

OUR PHOSPHORESCENCE IN CHRIST

I recently studied about colored diamonds, and found out some interesting things about them. I already knew that all diamonds have a crystalline structure; that is, their atoms are arranged in a particular pattern, making their chemical composition very regular and repeating, not random.[4] What I didn't know was that a *colored* diamond has a certain type of "defect" in its crystalline structure. A colored diamond has some kind of "impurity" in its chemical composition. This might be some extra atoms of hydrogen, nitrogen, or boron mixed into its pattern. These atoms affect the pattern, making it just a little less structured, a little less "perfect". This disruption of the pattern is what gives the colored diamond its unique hue. These diamonds are extremely valued and are more rare than their non-colored rock relatives. Colored diamonds also possess a property called *phosphorescence*. Phosphorescence is what makes a colored diamond glow a particular color, after it is exposed to ultraviolet light. These diamonds have a unique "fingerprint" depending on the color of their phosphorescence, and the duration (how long they continue to glow after being placed in the light).[5] The Hope Diamond, when exposed to UV light, glows bright fiery red, like a hot coal, for up to several minutes. The Portuguese Diamond is pale yellow in color, but glows bright blue after being in the light.[6]

Imagine yourself like one of these diamonds. Beautiful just the way you are, but radiantly glowing when exposed to the LIGHT of JESUS. If you allow the glory light of Christ to infiltrate your being, inside and out, you will experience a phosphorescence of your own. A beautiful, unique glow that outshines any seeming "flaws" that lie on or beneath the surface. When you look in the mirror, hold your reflection up against the light of the Lord Jesus, instead of the darkness of the world you live in. See what a difference *His* beauty makes in your spirit and soul. **Let *HIS perfection* be your true beauty!** See yourself the way He made you, the way He sees you. WONDERFULLY made!

"He has made everything beautiful..." Ecclesiastes 3:11 (AMP)

CHAPTER 11

HANDS THAT PROVIDE

"I will not forget you! See, I have engraved
you on the palms of my hands."
Isaiah 49:15-16 (NIV)

Money makes the world go 'round. At least that's what some people say. Others say *love* does that. I guess it's up for debate? There was a time when I thought I could "live on love". Then I tried doing that for quite a long while, and it turned out to be *much* trickier than it sounds. I know firsthand how a lack of cash for basic necessities, month after month, has a way of dampening the fires of love. I have seen what lack of money can do to people, what it has done to me. I've also seen what *too much* money does to people. Money is a curious thing. We need it. We want it. There never seems to be enough of it.

Growing up, I was well aware that money was not something that came easily to my parents. I was greatly fortunate to have parents who loved each other and didn't argue much. They were two people who were actually very good at "living on love". They made a habit of living below their means, and, in spite of that, they managed to stay united as a couple. That's no small feat by today's standards of norm. But the bank has a way of straining even the most unified of marriages. Whenever my parents *did* fight, the root of the argument was almost always *money*. It was always in such short supply. My parents would sit together regularly to "do the budget", and often this practice would end in some sort of turmoil with one or both of them either in tears or in some sort of frustrated upset....and grumpy. It's terribly hard to "do a budget" when there's no money to do it *with*, broke month after month, year after year. It's downright miserable if you let it be.

But despite their financial hardships, my parents found ways to give to many others as unto God. They regularly gave tithes and offerings to their church, missionaries, and needy people in their community and around the world. At our house, money was not something to live for. It was something to use for what you need, and then give the rest away. My parents' agenda did not center on the pursuit of money and *stuff*. In their minds, we needed enough money to live on, and whatever was left was our measure of means to do things for others. Once my father gathered our family together in the living room and gave us each a pair of scissors and a credit card. He asked us to cut up the cards and place them in a pile at the center of the room. He then taught us about what it means to depend on God instead of credit card companies. He warned us about the dangers of debt. He framed the pieces of the cards and hung them in his study, to remind us whenever we saw them (and probably to remind himself) that when times are hard, God will provide. And not by borrowing with interest. So we praised God for the ways He met our needs. If we ate peanut butter sandwiches, beans, and rice for days on end, we gave thanks because we were eating. The needs of other people were all around us, needs that often seemed much greater than our own.

I was six years old when I first crossed the Texas border into Mexico, where I would spend a lot of time from then through my teenage years. In Mexico I'd see children begging, dirty and shoeless and some of them blind, deaf, maimed, crippled. Men and women with deformed hands or feet, missing all or parts of their extremities, begging for money or selling trinkets and candies just to get by. In the mountains of Mexico, I saw families of six or more, living in "houses" as big as my bedroom, huts made entirely from sticks, with no doors, just openings to walk through. No flooring, just dirt. No running water, no electricity. Nothing. These places almost always smelled bad and the food was usually difficult for me to swallow. I and my family would return home from those Mexico trips, home to our very rudimentary apartment, home to our food bank meals, our hand-me-down clothing, and our thrift store furniture, knowing we were *blessed beyond measure*. This gave me a great deal of perspective even as a young girl. It made me care very little about monetary wealth. It made me feel pretty spoiled. It made me understand just how relative the word "poor" can really be. Perhaps our next-door neighbors viewed us as "poor", but then, what about those kids begging for pesos on the streets of Reynosa? Or the ones sleeping on the dirt floor out in the rancho? Were they not the *truly* poor ones? Those kids lived just a few miles from where I lived, but their world may as well have been a different planet.

This early repeated exposure to severe poverty gave me a deep concern for people living in destitute conditions, by no fault of their own. Whenever I saw images of sick and starving children in Africa or any other part of the world, I cried and felt sick to my stomach. I believed that God was taking care of *my* needs, but wondered, "Why isn't He taking care of *their* needs too?" I wanted so desperately to share with those kids what I had.

A lot has happened since then, to teach me about money and its use (and misuse) in the world. Much of this teaching I received when *I* was the one at the poverty end of the finance spectrum, when *I* was the one deeply in need and receiving help from some cheerful giver. Those times (some of which I will tell you about in this chapter and the next) were instrumental in showing me Who God is and part of what His purpose is for me while I am walking this earth. Sometimes I still cry and feel sick over the reality of so many people sick, hurting, and hungry in the world. It is heart-breaking. But I understand a few things now that I didn't understand as a child:

1. My desire to give to the needy has- all along- been <u>God's Spirit</u> compelling me to help. *The wrongs in the world are plentiful because of sin's pillaging effects. The Spirit of God speaks to us about which wrongs <u>we can right</u>, individually. Our responses to His voice are often half-hearted and selfish; or we ignore Him altogether because we have other things to do, other ways we prefer to spend our money and time. But when we <u>do</u> respond the right way, we change for the good, we are blessed, and bona fide miracles ensue.*

2. The basic needs of people in the world are not going unmet because God doesn't love them, but because too few <u>people</u> love them enough to do anything about it. *Many folks <u>are</u> intentionally loving the world, purposely "being the change". But many are NOT. Just as God gives us the free will to choose His salvation gift, He gives us free will concerning how much we are really going to do for others. He shows us what the needs are. But it's our decision to help or not. Deciding not to help is falling short of our life purpose; it's wasting our lives, really. Deciding to help reaps reward both in this life and in eternity.*

God has revealed Himself, in profound ways over and over again, as my PROVIDER. He has taken care of me and my family. Usually His gifts have been the result of *His followers'* obedience. The arms of the Lord are extended toward me and they are full of good things, necessary things, which I could not obtain on my own. This financial provision has been miraculous. It's made me depend on Him and appreciate Him. I've learned contentment and what it means to give, from many friends and even from a few strangers.

One of the first people who taught me about God's provision was Mrs. Chavez...

MRS. CHAVEZ

At ten years old, I was baptized in a Hispanic Baptist church, in a poor neighborhood in South Texas. The congregation was almost entirely Mexican American, Spanish-speaking people whose lives had been transformed by Jesus Christ. They met in a small old house that had been converted to a church sanctuary. The man who baptized me spent all of his time giving to the poor. He and his wife spent their days picking up food from grocery stores and delivering it to homes in the community. When they delivered the food, they would tell the recipients that Jesus loved them, and that He died for them. They prayed for them if they wanted prayer, and then invited them to this neighborhood church, where there was always singing and baptizing and people's lives were being changed.

In every service, a little old woman in a wheelchair would come to the front altar area, with her harmonica. And she would play a hymn. Mrs. Chavez had not had an easy life. She'd endured at least one stroke, perhaps several, which left her feeble and partially paralyzed. Her speech was slurred. Facial paralysis made her mouth crooked and her smile broken, but still she was always smiling! And she played that harmonica so well. Sometimes she struggled to stand while playing her song, and before she played, usually in tears, she talked about what the song meant to her. It was always something about God's goodness to her, of the faithful ways He was helping her and meeting her needs.

I sometimes felt very sorry for Mrs. Chavez, but usually I just admired her. There was something very special about her getting up to do this time after time. I'd sometimes complain about going to that little Spanish church, because my friends attended other churches, churches with plush carpet and comfortable seats, grand pianos and cool music. Churches with big youth groups and air conditioning. But the paralyzed Mrs. Chavez playing *Great Is Thy Faithfulness* on her harmonica would bring me right out of my self-pity pretty quickly. I now understand fully what she already knew all those years ago:

> *God is providing for me, and He always will.*
> *It's my purpose to help others so they will see God's provision too.*

GEORGE MUELLER MOMENTS

I think Mrs. Chavez had experienced some George Mueller moments in her life. That's the term I use for moments when much-needed provision comes with no explanation of where it came. No explanation besides HEAVEN, that is! When I was young, I read about George Mueller and his England orphanage. I pictured in my mind the story playing out: all the little orphan kids sitting at a long wooden table, hungry and ready to eat, praying, asking God to send them food. And Mr. Mueller there, announcing to the children that he is going to pray until God provides food for them. And then he prays with the power of God's Spirit on him, with trust and hope in his heart, not stopping until that moment- that loud knock on the orphanage door. And on the other side of it, bags of food. Enough food to supply them all with full tummies. As a little girl, I thought that was the coolest story ever! I believed it really happened. I had no reason to doubt it could. And now, thirty years later, I not only believe it really happened, but I can tell you it happened TO ME...

It was a winter evening, a Friday night. I was at home with my husband and children. Completely broke but enjoying being together, we were fully aware it was going to be an interesting weekend, with no money in the bank, no gas in the car, hardly any food in the fridge or cupboards. I had taken inventory of what we had, and I knew we would have enough to get through the weekend if we rationed. Monday might be tricky, but we just needed to make it to Tuesday. Tuesday was payday. I asked God to help us keep the right perspective until Tuesday, to help us appreciate all that we did have.

Around 9:30 P.M. I heard a knock on our apartment door. *"Who would be here at this time of night?"* I thought to myself. *"It's probably the police coming to inquire about something that's happened at our apartment complex."* There were always shady characters around our apartment complex. Lots of trouble. When I looked out the peephole, I saw no one at the door. *"Whoever it was must have had the wrong apartment, or it's some loser playing a trick on us"*, I thought. But I opened the door anyway. No one was around. But there in the dingy, poorly-lit entry way, sat a cardboard box full of food goods. Several cans of Chef Boyardee and canned corn and green beans. Boxed Hamburger Helper, pasta and sauce, and some potatoes. I'll never forget how that food box sat there, looking up at me, as if to say, "Here I am!" I went quickly down the stairs to see who had dropped it there, but I saw no one. Not even a car driving off. It was as though the box just appeared. But not out of nowhere. Out of *heaven*!

That is not the only time I experienced that. There have been MANY times. Like at college when I went to the business office to make a payment on my school bill, and learned that my balance was $500.00 less than I thought, because someone had made an anonymous payment on my account. Or finding money in my school post office box so I could buy laundry soap and Ramen noodles and gas for my van. The van I got when a person I hardly knew called me at school to tell me he was giving me a vehicle, because he wanted to bless my family. Or the time I heard that my children would get to continue another year in Christian school, with their way almost entirely paid. Or the Christmas Eve when we received a box of gifts on our doorstep. *These* are some of my George Mueller moments.

But there are also altar-making moments...

CHAPTER 12

WATERY HANDS

"He who believes in Me- who cleaves to and trusts in and relies on Me- from his innermost being shall flow continuously springs and rivers of living water."
- Jesus, in John 7:38 (AMP)

There have been many times when I wanted to stop and make an altar to God. Just like they did in the Old Testament. Just stop what I'm doing and gather rocks to set down in a certain place, in memoriam of His revelation to me. Noah made an altar, after witnessing (and surviving) the most destructive natural disaster in the history of Earth...after being "cooped up" with his family and all those animals in the giant ark... then emerging from it so many months later, safely onto dry land.[1] Abraham, after receiving the promise that God would give the land of Canaan to him and his descendents, stopped and made an altar right in the place where God spoke to Him. The altar spot was a place to thank God, to praise Him for what He was doing and what He was going to do. It was also a place of memorial to return to later, a place to remember again that time when God showed Himself real, a place to talk to

Him. (Genesis 12:6-9; 13:4) Abraham's son Isaac made an altar after the Lord confirmed to him that He was still with him and that his life was being blessed. (Genesis 26:24-25) Jacob and Moses, David, Elijah, and many others made altars too. Special places to praise God and to remember He was with them. *I get why they did that!* They had received direct communication from heaven that *they were not forgotten.* And so have I...

PARKING LOT ALTARS

One evening, I found myself associating with Old Mother Hubbard. My kitchen cupboards were bare. As was my fridge. And my wallet. And my bank account. Our bills were pretty much paid and we had a little gas in the car. But payday was over a week away. I don't remember what I fixed that evening for our family to eat, but I remember that after it was gone, all we had left was a small bag of frozen squash and a head of broccoli. And no means to buy anything else.

That night we went to our usual mid-week service at church. A guest speaker had come to share a message about Elijah. He preached a powerful message about the time that God told Elijah to go to the wilderness brook during the terrible drought. There Elijah had water to drink every day, and a group of ravens came to him, in obedience to God's command. The ravens brought meat for Elijah to eat each morning and evening (I Kings 17).

After church that night, I wanted to ask our church friends if we could take some food from the church pantry. My husband Mark said to me, "No. Not yet. Let's pray awhile. God knows our need. He will provide." At first I didn't like that answer. Maybe my husband was embarrassed for anyone to know we had no food. Maybe he was wanting to trust God for a miracle. Either way, it wasn't easy for me to be patient. But we went home and we went to bed that night praying, with Elijah and his ravens on our minds. We didn't tell anyone but God how needy we were.

The next day began the same way, with prayer, as I went to

school for my usual workday. I was in the school office doing something after school, when a friend came in and asked if I had my car at school that day. "Yes," I replied, thinking, *"Did something happen to my car?"* She said reassuringly, "We have something to give you; could we put it in your car now?"

"Sure," I said, "Let me go get my key and I'll meet you out there."

When I got to my car, I saw my friend's car parked next to mine. The trunk was opened to expose bags of groceries, *quite a few bags of groceries.* Another friend was with her.

"Pop that trunk," they said, as they began unloading the bags to place them into my trunk. Looking at those two women of God and all the bags of groceries, I began to sob. The kind of sobbing that makes your shoulders move, the kind that feels like your insides are being emptied out of you. I was overcome with emotion over what I was seeing! I put my arms around them both and wept with relief. I told them we had nothing. I told them I'd been praying and was going to fast and pray until God provided. I told them, *"Nobody knew we needed this except for God."* I could have made an altar right there in the parking lot.

By now, my two friends were also shedding tears and confirming that this was indeed a work of God. They handed me a gift card for the local grocery store. "Whatever you need that isn't in these bags, you use this and go get it." When I got home and brought the bags up the apartment stairs into our kitchen, Mark saw the gift we'd been given and *he* began to weep. And we prayed *prayers of gratitude* as we and our two children unpacked the groceries, almost ceremoniously, giving thanks for every item, knowing full well that God had worked a miracle for us. God had provided.

Another time, in a different parking lot a few days before Thanksgiving (2007), I was approached by a co-worker after school. At the time, I didn't know her. All I really knew of her was her name. She was always friendly to me, but we rarely came in contact with one another. Just out of the blue, she informed me that her family wanted to help my family to have a nice Christmas. At first I thought she might mean they would give us a turkey or ham or something like that. But she proceeded to say, "If you could make a list of things your family needs, and things your children want for Christmas, and things you all like to have to eat and drink at Christmas, and when you might like to get a Christmas tree....well, just write it down and we are going to help you however we can." I remember not knowing what to say, except to ask, "Are you serious?" or "Is this for real?" and I found out she was QUITE serious. We received many gifts that Christmas, far in abundance of what we could have imagined. At the time, Mark was only getting part-time hours at his job pouring concrete, due to wet weather. (You can't pour concrete in steady rain, and it had been raining continuously every day for weeks.) We didn't know how we'd pay the December electric bill, much less for Christmas treats and new toys for the kids. God had provided.

MEDICAL OFFICE ALTARS

Several years without dental insurance caught up with our family in a big way a few years ago. Even though we had been caring for our teeth well, we could not afford regular dental check-ups and cleanings. And so we came to discover that our daughter Hannah was in need of several fillings, three extractions (one of them permanent), and a root canal. I remember the day I found out about that. Realizing the amount of dental work she would need to have done, I sat weeping, completely overwhelmed- not only by the thought of the expense- but by the knowledge that Hannah's dental problems were the result of being so "broke" all the time. That was heart-breaking.

I pulled it together and called a dentist, explaining that my daughter's need was urgent, and that I would pay what I could and use a credit card or make payments on the remaining balance. I was prepared to pay out of pocket, even if it meant having nothing left that month for gas and bills. I just wanted Hannah to be cared for.

The dentist took us right in, helped Hannah, and then before we were ready to check out, an office manager called me in to the office and sat me down to discuss the treatment plan. I remember feeling on the verge of tears, still trying to hold it together. *"How in the world am I going to pay for this?"*, I thought. *"I'm going to have to get a different job, or a second job..."* I wasn't praying really. I was just worrying.

Then I heard these words from the office manager's mouth:

"We want to provide all of your family's dental care at no cost to you."

WHAT?!? Did I just hear what I think I heard??

"Yes, we are going to provide the dental treatments for Hannah, and all your family, including you and your husband, free of charge. We sometimes do this for families who are uninsured. We want to do it for your family this time."

I began to cry. I could not control my emotion. This was so unexpected! But I knew it was God's doing. He was providing for us *again*! He was easing my doubting, troubled mind. He was making it so I wouldn't have to bear the burden of debt or find another job. WOW. I was blown away! I vowed right then never to forget how it felt sitting in that dentist office chair, being told that our needs were going to be met in this way. God increased my faith, you see, in a way I will never forget. He showed me His *providing* hands.

In that same year and in years to follow, we received many other gifts like that. Excellent medical care for my husband Mark. Discounts on MRI's and medicines. God even provided 6 months of Kaiser medical insurance for me, completely free of charge, through a charity organization. I had developed a nasal hemangioma (a benign tumor of blood vessels) which was surgically removed in those months, *at no cost to me*. How does this happen? I believe it is GOD, looking after me! These big blessing events have not been trivially important in my life. With each one, I felt like I may as well have won the lottery! Only this wasn't luck. It was much better than luck. It was love.

Another time I was at work, struggling to push through the pain of an illness that had come on, about a week before. A severe cough was exhausting me and causing me to sleep poorly at night. I was pretty sure I had bronchitis or maybe even pneumonia. I needed to see a doctor, but I didn't have the money. I didn't even have enough money for Nyquil or cough drops. I had been praying to God for a few days, asking Him to take my sickness away. After school, I received a note with a simple "God bless you" message, with a $100.00 bill. I had not told anyone I didn't have money for the doctor. In fact, I had been downplaying my sickness in front of others, so I would not appear weak. But there it was. The money I needed for the doctor visit. So I went that day. The whole time I was waiting, and getting my chest x-ray, and filling my prescriptions, I was very aware of Who was looking out for me. I told some of the medical office staff about my miracle that day. And now I'm telling you. So you can see that the blessing of the Lord is real. See it in your life! Recognize *your* good gifts as His provision. He is taking care of you because He loves you so much!

GAS PUMP ALTARS

On two other occasions, years apart and in different states, God showed me He is still providing oil in miraculous ways, as He did for the widow women in I Kings 17 and I Kings 4. The first woman had only enough oil left to make a small meal for herself and her son, and then she would face starvation. But God replenished her cruse of oil as she used it, so it did not run empty. The second widow woman had only one thing of value to her name: a jar of oil. God told her, through Elisha, to go borrow empty jars from her neighbors, then come back home and use her jar to fill up those other jars. Miraculously, she did that and was able to sell all the extra oil to make a living and to keep her sons from being sold as slaves. Of course, my situation was not as dire as that. But my situation was bad enough to cause me stress and bring me to my knees in prayer. On these two particular occasions, I was completely out of money and my car was running on fumes. No gasoline and no means to buy more. Both of these times, I was at work getting ready to ask someone for a ride to and from work the next day (knowing I wouldn't have enough gas to get there and back), when I checked my "incoming mail" box to find an envelope with cash inside. No note, no name to say who it was from, just an envelope with my name on it with money inside. At the gas pump on those days, I was so impressed by the way God was still multiplying oil in miraculous ways, this time for ME! My cruse of oil had not failed. God had shown Himself real again.

THE RICHES OF HIS LOVE

Even writing this book has been a lesson in provision.

When I decided to write this book, it was toward the end of the summer of 2011. I had lost my job at the start of that summer, and my teacher salary would be ending in August. I'd been job-hunting, but had no offers, and I was not sure which direction to go yet. We had purchased our home only 7 months before. We knew it would be very difficult to pay our mortgage without some divine intervention. I went to a special worship service at a church near my home, to bring my heavy heart before my Savior, and to hear from Him. I was about to enter the first full month without a regular paycheck. Times had been hard enough even with the paycheck. I had no idea how we would keep up financially. I was worried and I was so tired. I needed spiritual refreshment. I needed time to think. In the back of my mind, I wanted so badly to take a little time to start writing this story.

That night after spending some time in prayerful song, after my heart had been completely opened to the Word of God, after distractions had been cleared away, the pastor read from Revelation 1. As he spoke, I was praying for direction about what to do. And we got to the end of the chapter, the part when God tells John that He was showing Him things, things about Himself and His glory, and He wanted John to write them down. Reading these verses, I

KNEW God was directing me. It was pretty obvious! Here is what I read:

> *"I am the Alpha and Omega. The First and the Last. Write promptly what you see, in a book. Do not be afraid! I am the Ever-Living One! I am living in the eternity of eternities! Write the things you see- what they are and (what they) signify."* *(Revelation 1:11, 17-19 AMP)*

It was in those moments while reading those verses, hearing from Jesus, that I decided to start writing down my story that very night. I felt so excited, so in love with Jesus for showing me these words. I couldn't wait to get started. But there was still that little part of me that doubted, that wondered how this was actually going to work. *"How will our mortgage be paid if I don't work full time? How will we get by?"* In the next moments, we were standing to sing the song *Forever Reign*, by Hillsong United.[2] The song speaks of running to Jesus' arms. Feeling His embrace. Seeing His light. Recognizing His Kingship. And it declares to Him, in prayerful tone, *"The riches of Your love will always be enough."*

As I stood singing those words, Jesus was telling me to just *love* Him. To just see HIM- *only HIM*- in those moments, and stop worrying about bills and money. He was telling me to share with whomever I could, about His goodness and love and grace and forgiveness and healing. He was telling me that HE WAS ENOUGH! He was all I needed! *"You can pay our mortgage, Jesus? Really?"* I was hearing, *"Forget about that. Just love Me, and receive my love."* In those moments I felt His love filling the room and filling me. I was crying a relieved cry. I knew we'd be OK. I stopped worrying.

Just a few days later, I was organizing some files in our house and came across some papers from our house purchase. This brought me to remember that at the time of our closing, the bank lender had given us one year of a "mortgage protection plan", free of cost to us. This plan provided 100% of the mortgage payment, for up to 6 months, IF an unexpected loss of employment came to us within one year of the home purchase. *"**This** is how You're going to do it!"* I exclaimed before God. At a time when we may have otherwise faced foreclosure on a home we hadn't lived in for even one year, God saw fit to pay our mortgage <u>completely</u> for us, for several months. He was telling us, "Keep your home. Use it for My glory and make it a home of love. Share it with others. Use it to bless people. This home is part of my plan for you. I am abiding there with you, and I have everything under control, so don't worry. I'm all you need."

In those months, some things that had broken down in our own home and family could be rebuilt. I could sing, I could write, I could *think*. I could spend time with the family. I really did need some time to "push the reset button", and God was giving it to me! I could cook healthy meals and exercise more. I finished my Master's degree and got my teaching certificate. Two years later, I was offered a permanent position teaching high school science. That was another miracle of many things weaving together to set me down in exactly the right place at the right time. The Heavenly Father's provision- again- *not lacking*.

I choose to believe that the events I have described are not a collection of coincidences. They are direct personal evidences of this loving Father telling His daughter, "I'm all you need." And showing me that part of my purpose here is to meet the needs of other people, in His name. That they may also see Him and believe they are loved. Every time we give to someone in the name of the Lord, we are being His hands, His fingers. That others may look at us and see Him.

In Isaiah 40:12 (NKJV) God's greatness is described. This verse describes His hand as holding all the water on the earth. He has "measured the waters in the hollow of His hand." I love imagining all the oceans and rivers and streams right in the big, bright hand of God! What a symbol of His care for us! We know that water is vital to life on Earth. Our most basic need, water sustains us.

Without it, we die. Quickly. God has given us not only the physical water we need for drinking, but the spiritual life water to keep us going for all eternity! That same mighty hand of the Lord, the hand that's able to hold all the waters, is extended to hold OUR hands. "I the Lord your God hold your right hand! Fear not; I will help you!" (Isaiah 41:13 AMP) And then the outpouring comes, from His hand to ours:

> *"The poor and needy are seeking water; their tongues are parched with thirst. I the Lord will answer them; I, the God of Israel, will not forsake them. I will open rivers on the bare heights, and fountains in the midst of the valleys. I will make the wilderness a pool of water, and the dry land springs of water. That men may see and know and consider and understand together that the hand of the Lord has done this, that the Holy One of Israel has created it." (Isaiah 41:17-18, 20; AMP)*

The hands of God have poured water upon my life.
The Giver of water for us to drink...
the Giver of oil...
He is the Giver of all good things!

CHAPTER 13

ARMS THAT EMBRACE ME

*"I can feel His left hand under my head,
and His right hand embraces me.
I am my beloved's, and His desire is toward me!"*
Song of Solomon 2:6 & 7:10 (AMP)

Marriage is a beautiful thing. When it works like it's supposed to. When it doesn't, it's quite the opposite of beautiful. It's downright ugly. Hideous at times. Marriage has a way of bringing out a person's selfishness. Or selflessness. Success in marriage has much to do with which one of those traits the wife and husband choose to demonstrate. While selfishness in one or both partners can spawn ugliness in a marriage relationship, self*less*ness can restore great beauty to it. I have learned the most about the character of Jesus through my marriage. These things I have learned not just in the blissful times, when everything was all daisies and rainbows and flute music being played by baby cherubs sitting on puffy clouds in a sunny sky. Although those happy times have had their special place in showing me a part of who Christ Jesus is, the times when Jesus has shown Himself the *most* vividly were times when my marriage was the most fragile, the most brittle. The times when I thought it was not going to survive.

When I married Mark in 1996, I was completely crazy about him. He was my whole world, and I do believe I was his. Together we felt we could do anything, conquer any adversity. Our love would carry us through *anything*. Mark was full of strength, vitality, life. He was like no man I'd ever met. Completely intriguing. Adventurous, spontaneous, with just enough crazy in him to make things never boring when we were together. He was just enough of a tough guy to be really impressive without being a jerk. And it was easy to imagine him as an amazing father to a couple of bouncing babies.

I felt like Mark and I were made for each other. I felt like he was my gift from God. When we were dating, we went on all kinds of adventures together. I called him my Alaska mountain man, because that's what he *was*. He showed me beautiful Alaska, taught me how to fish, how to drive a stick shift, how to drive on snowy roads and frozen lakes in the winter. We shared morning walks in the woods, afternoon naps on warm river banks, and 2 a.m. breakfasts at our favorite open-all-night restaurant. There was always so much to talk about, so much to share. But to me, the best parts of our relationship were the talks we had about God and the Bible. Our talks would last well into the middle of the night, talks about the Old Testament, prophecy, eschatology, theology. We studied Scripture together. Mark impressed me with his zeal for the Bible and for Christ. Before long we found ourselves sharing dreams of ministry, and soon our dreams merged into *one* dream. When we got engaged, our whole relationship was centered around one dream: to be missionaries together. To use our gifts to the fullest, together, to do something BIG for God, to really live our lives as one. This was the plan.

My Honeymoon Groom

So, when we got married, I was one excited happy camper, as you can imagine. Not only had I met the man of my dreams, but we were going to be MISSIONARIES together! I was thrilled, overjoyed. I thought I could not possibly love Mark any more than I did then. My heart was filled to bursting with love. In our most tender, intimate times, parts of the Bible that I never understood before- like most of the Song of Solomon- began to make sense. I was completely infatuated- even obsessed- with this wonderful person I had married. I knew he was not perfect, but he was perfect in my eyes at that time. I remember the continuous realization, that THIS was the level of love Jesus felt for me. WOW, what a LOVE! This crazy, pursuing, all-consuming love, an unstoppable force of passion. The kind of love that makes you forget everyone and everything else besides your lover. The kind of love that drives away fear and warms you completely, accepts you completely, desires you *completely.*

As I became more and more aware of what our marriage bond meant- physically, spiritually, mentally- I marveled at this love I was experiencing, and what it represented in the spiritual realm. I *understood* so much better now, why God intended sex just for marriage. Sex represents the exclusive, unique oneness we have with Christ when we give ourselves completely to Him as He gave Himself completely for us. The powerful unity, the bond, the fulfillment that is meant to come from a sexual relationship- is a depiction of how deeply and completely GOD loves us. He knows us fully and He wants us to know *Him* fully, and to enjoy His gifts in an atmosphere of absolute trust and safety. When sex is diminished to "just a physical act", or -worse- when it is diminished even further to an act of lustful selfishness, it is used for a purpose completely opposite of that which was intended by its Creator. God did not create sex to be a weapon of abuse or a tool of manipulation or abandonment. Man's sin turned it into that. Sex is supposed to be entirely about giving one's self to another person, not taking something from another person. It is meant to be a picture of divine love. Sin has twisted it into a picture of lewdness and greed. Our world has embraced a "take what you can get" outlook about sex, which has distorted it beyond recognition from what it is actually meant to be.

In the sweetest times when I felt the most cherished by Mark early in our marriage union, I thanked the Lord of heaven for showing me this higher level of love that I could not have comprehended before. I thanked God often for His gift of marriage sex, knowing it *was* a picture of His love for me, and a key way that our marriage could bring honor to Him. Through my loving Mark and his loving me, God was revealing things about *HIS* love to me. I understood more about the peace and joy found in God (Who is love Himself) for all eternity, the security and favor we have in the presence of Jesus, the One Who loves us unreservedly and unconditionally. In those first years married to Mark, I came to deeply know what it meant to be entirely "sick with love", what it meant for my heart to be completely "ravished" (Song of Solomon 2:5; 4:9). Through my earthly marriage relationship, I was sampling the heavenly connection which my Savior wants to have with me, forever. In times when we drew the closest together, Mark and I were drawing closer to God too. We thanked God openly and often, for bringing us together and for giving us this taste of His love for us. It truly was fragrant and sweet like honey; astoundingly beautiful beyond anything mankind could ever create. Like vast gardens of roses and herbs among tall, sweet-smelling trees surrounded with precious gem stones (Song of Solomon 5). Jesus showed me His perfect *love* in those first years. I was seeing parts of His character- depths of His love- that I could not see before. I thought I had arrived at the "highest level" of love; that it could not go any higher or deeper. I was wrong.

THE DEATH THAT BREATHES LIFE

At that time, I would have given my life for Mark, without giving a moment's thought about it. I would sometimes imagine myself in some life-or-death situation, where I would have to give my life for Mark. And I knew that because I would die in his place, without thinking twice about it, then I must be *truly* in love with him. I romanticized what it would be like to "die for Mark". It would look something like that ending scene in the movie *Titanic*, when Jack gives up his spot on the floating wood board, for Rose.[1] It would be so touching, so beautiful. Since then, I've grown up a lot. And God has shown me that "giving your life" for your spouse *is* indeed a big part of what *every* beautiful working marriage is about. Dying for your spouse is what *every* beautiful "working" marriage is about. But *not* in the way I originally thought. The dying is actually done progressively over time, not all at once. The dying is done voluntarily and unconditionally. It is not a physical death; it is a death to one's selfish desires. A death to one's <u>flesh</u>. The apostle Paul spoke of this in Romans 8:13. God has shown me this Scripture verse with direct relation to my marriage with Mark, and it goes like this: "If you live according to the dictates of your own flesh (your own carnal desires and selfish preferences), your marriage relationship will surely die. But if, through the power of God's Holy Spirit, you habitually put to death the evil deeds prompted by your body, your marriage relationship will remain alive and vibrant throughout your life." This does *not* mean a person ought not to desire anything and should only live to please the spouse. It *does* mean that selfless sacrifice is exalted above selfish actions when it comes to relationships. *Death to your flesh breathes life into your marriage!*

I didn't really understand this fully until I was faced with the decision to die to myself -again and again- or let my marriage die. You see, in reality, dying for Mark hasn't been "romantic" at all. It's been a gritty, sometimes frightening uphill journey. But I would make the journey again in a heartbeat. Because in that struggle, in choosing to live life in a dying-to-flesh process, Jesus has shown Himself to me as my true Groom. My honeymoon Groom, but so much more beyond that. Choosing to give up things we want, out of love for another person, is not easy- even when our love for that person is immense. But when we make that choice, we demonstrate Christ's likeness to the world. And then we are able to see more clearly, *what He did for us*, and what He is doing for us even *now*, and what He *will do* for us in the future.

MY NEED MEETER GROOM

One of my favorite memories from our wedding ceremony was during our exchange of vows. A few days before the wedding, our attending pastor met with us to review with us the set of pre-written vows we could use if we liked them. He read them with us, and we did agree to use them in the ceremony, except for one. There was a part where Mark was supposed to say to me, "Davida, I will try to meet your needs." Mark didn't like that.

"I don't want to promise to try to meet Davida's needs," Mark confidently told the pastor. "I want to promise to meet them. Please remove the word 'try' when you read these vows during the ceremony."

The pastor agreed and scribbled something down on his note sheet. I thought that was quite bold and noble of my husband-to-be, especially seeing as we had just read the fabulous book *His Needs, Her Needs* by Willard F. Harley, Jr.[2]

A few days later, during our actual ceremony, our pastor did not make the change. Instead, he read it the way it had originally been written.

"Davida, I will try to meet your needs,"

to which Mark repeated,

"Davida I *will* meet your needs."

I don't think everyone in the audience caught the word drop. But *I* did. Mark said it so intently, so deliberately. He said it as a promise should be said: with resolve, with the utmost sincere intentions of following through. For as long as we both shall live.

Mark and I did not predict that some external factor would ever affect his ability to keep that promise to me. We did not know that a time would come when Mark could not meet my every need. How could we have known that Mark was making a promise that was impossible to keep?

Fast forward to 10 years later....

We were living in South Texas, where we had moved with the hope of doing mission work in Mexico. Things went well there at first. After spending a few years in California, unintentionally straying away from God, ministry, and each other, we were eager and excited to get back to what was most important. Optimistic and united in our goals for the future, we were content and excited just to be a family. We traveled along the Mexico-Texas border doing Christian outreaches and were involved in youth leadership and ministering to the elderly. Mark and I were really going after our dream of being in full-time Christian ministry together. But struggles were growing in number and magnitude seemingly by the day. Unpaid debts, lack of steady income, health limitations, and a harsh climate made it difficult to accomplish what we had set out to do. We believed God wanted us to be missionaries, but doors seemed to remain closed to us. At the time we were spiritually and physically strong, spending hours daily studying the Word of God and ministry methods. We ate healthy foods and exercised, earnestly preparing ourselves for whatever God wanted us to do. We felt SO very ready to give all our time and energy to mission work. But that plane just couldn't seem to lift off the ground. Mark had a hard time finding work in South Texas, knowing little Spanish, and the heat exhausted him terribly. He enrolled in truck driving school, thinking he could drive for a living temporarily, drive us right out of debt, and we could still do ministry together when he came home. We would both work jobs for a time, pay off our debts, save money, and then we'd try again. That was the plan.

Mark was home about six days over the course of the next six months.

And thus began the spiritual breakdown which would later try to destroy our family unity.

Each time that Mark came home from trucking, he was noticeably weaker spiritually, physically, and emotionally. He began losing the momentum he'd gained with his health in the months prior, as he was now eating fast food from the truck stops, and getting almost no exercise, day after day. Not only that, when he was on the road, he was alone almost all of the time. The only people he encountered were dispatchers on his truck's computer and the people hanging out at the truck stops. He became very lonely and depressed. We tried to make sense of it, thinking maybe God was calling us to be involved in a ministry for truckers. But that didn't seem like a good fit, either. The last time he came home, Mark quit his job with the trucking company, deciding he'd try to drive locally instead. But week after week, no job, no job. He began spiraling downward. He lost his motivation for ministry. He told me he felt spiritually dead. He said he didn't know God anymore. And his actions backed up those statements. I was devastated.

Mark stopped doing many of the things he used to do. He changed so rapidly before my eyes, and nothing I did could make things go back to normal. Financial hardship pushed us to the edge of bankruptcy, and Mark began feeling responsible for that. He sustained a few injuries, and a recurring infection caused him to be very ill a lot of the time. He turned to alcohol more and more often, to numb himself from the pain of the course of his life (which was also *my* life). I resented that *immensely*. In a short time, things grew worse. He talked about killing himself. He slept a lot. His depression bred a raging anger that led him into some poor decisions, each one causing him to slip further into depression and feelings of worthlessness. Weeks went by like this. A wedge was forming between us, and it grew larger with time. I was not proud of Mark any more. I *wanted* to be. But I wasn't. I was disappointed in him, hurt, and frustrated. But I still had a glimmer of hope that somehow things would get back to good for us.

In October 2006, almost exactly 10 years after vowing to meet my needs, Mark left me and the kids in Texas to head for Washington state, to try and regain some stability emotionally and to get a good job. I had been functioning on my own while he was trucking; I could do it again, temporarily. Besides, I was teaching under contract at a great school where both of our children were attending and very happy. It seemed best that we remain in Texas until my contract was fulfilled. Mark would find work up north, and we would join him when the school year was completed. That seemed the best workable plan.

And so, we were separated again, this time for seven *more* months. We got to visit Mark for *two weeks* during that stretch.

I began functioning more independently from my husband. We were still very much "together in spirit", but because of the distance between us, things were weird for awhile. We didn't have the cohesiveness we'd enjoyed in the past. We only talked by phone or text. Web cam conversations allowed for better talks toward the end of that time. But we were growing apart. The groom of my honeymoon, though still my lover, had tried desperately hard to meet my every need. But in those months, I was beginning to understand that Mark was *not* going to always be able to meet my every need as I once thought he could. God was showing me that <u>HE</u> was the One Who would always meet my needs. <u>ALL</u> of them. Not just my physical and financial needs, as I described in the last two chapters, but my deep need for close companionship, for relational intimacy.

There were many times that year when I would have felt utterly entirely alone, if not for God. *God* was the One I talked to as I was going to sleep every night, the One I talked to when I woke up in the morning. He was the One I began calling on the most. I needed Him; I needed His counsel. I had many responsibilities in and out of the home. Our children were ages 5 and 7. I had a lot of trouble accepting where I was and what I was doing; just the whole situation. God *helped me to accept it* and to see past my own self-pity. In my darkest nights of loneliness and bitterness that year, God spoke back to me just as I spoke to Him. He showed me so many new things in His Word. He showed me what contentment really looks like (a lesson I would need to learn again a few years later). He showed me what PATIENCE really is. And SERVICE. He showed me the importance of doing TODAY'S WORK TODAY, instead of always dwelling on "the next step" or the future I kept envisioning for myself.

HEAVEN'S HUG

Those months were the very beginning of a long, winding pilgrimage which I would take- no longer being held continuously each day in my earthly husband's arms, but in *Jesus'* arms, which would come around me stronger and tighter than I'd ever felt them. One particular encounter stands out most vividly in my mind...

In extended worship service one evening, after singing for an hour only to God, I began to feel like He and I were the only ones in the room. When the worship time had started, I was feeling completely alone- so husbandless, so painfully aware of my solitude, standing in a crowded room but not next to anyone I knew or that knew me. But as I began singing- and continued singing- in an attitude of gratitude, praying to my Savior Who loved me so perfectly, EVERYTHING and EVERYONE ELSE *faded away* in those moments, and HE was the ONLY ONE on my mind. The ONLY ONE I was giving my heart to in those moments. Just like during those moments of tender closeness and intimacy in my marriage. As I sang to my Savior and poured my heart out to Him, crying through the song lyrics, I wanted to give Him every part of me. I felt like reaching up for Him. I had NEVER BEFORE raised my hands in church. But this time, I was compelled to reach up in my adoration, in my broken thankfulness. And when I did that, I felt so incredibly warm! Not because of an uncomfortable warmth, but a *comforting* one, like how it feels to be at the beach on a clear, sunny day with the sunshine beaming right down on you. It felt like warm light, covering me from my outstretched hands to my feet. I felt light, like I was rising up. I couldn't reach high enough. My arms were in the air a long time, but they did not grow sore. And then I felt a pressure, just like a hug, wrapping around me. Exactly like a blanket. Still adoring Him in my song, I remained there with my arms fully raised, still crying, still reaching, still thanking and loving, still basking in that warmth, His light. And I knew that *the Lord was hugging me.* That might sound weird to you, but I'm telling you- that's exactly how it felt; like a warm, tingly, tight, wonderfully close hug. *I needed that so much.* He was meeting my need!

You see, *God was bringing me into His arms of love* in that lonely time of my life. When my husband's gentle, loving hands were miles away from me- and had been for many months- GOD'S hand was there under my head, giving me peaceful rest and security in the midst of what could have been a very turbulent time. He was making me *strong* in spite of my disappointments and struggles. I was now able to *see* HIM not only as my Honeymoon Groom, but as my Need Meeter Groom. I knew He would always take care of me, and I would never have to feel alone again. *What an incredible love He gives!*

I don't know what your outlook of romantic love is. Maybe it's something you have plenty of. Maybe it's something you're fed up with, because it has only ever disappointed or betrayed you somehow. Maybe you have not known it yet, but you desperately want to. Maybe it's something you once knew, but lost.

If you are enjoying marital love the way it was designed to be enjoyed, thank the Lord for that! Honor Him in that, and let Him keep showing you a living picture of something very heavenly, something eternal! If you are reading this never having been married, or having been in a marriage that ended for whatever reason, it does not mean God loves you any less! He loves you just as much as anyone happily married. *He is ready to embrace you and give you all the pure love you desire!* Talk to God in your solitude, in your loneliness. Tell Him what you need (even though He already knows) and He will be there to meet you in your prayer! Read His Word. Listen intently to what it tells you; apply it to every tough situation in your relationships. Wait for Him and let Him *show* you what He has in mind for you at this time in your life. He will reveal great things to you!

If you're reading this and you are in an unhappy, unloving time of marriage, don't give up! If your marriage failed or ended, whether you wanted it to or not, leaving you fractured in some way, take heart! Let Christ Jesus fill in every gap, every empty void that exists in your soul because of a spouse leaving you physically or emotionally. The Lord of heaven is a never-ending wellspring of love, waiting for you to come to Him and raise your arms to touch Him. He will touch you- just as He touched me- and He can give you all the love you need. You are *never alone* with Him beside you, below you, above you, all around you, taking you into His open, loving arms.

"Love waved as a protecting and comforting banner over my head when I was near Him." Song of Solomon 2:4 (AMP)

CHAPTER 14

FIERY HANDS

*"The Messenger of God's promises (Jesus) is like a blazing
fire refining precious metal. Like a refiner of silver, He
will closely watch as the dross is burned away. He will
purify the ministers of God, so that they will do their
work for God with pure hearts." Malachi 3:1-4 (TLB)*

A Shakespearean tragedy is called a tragedy because some
catastrophe occurs which sets the story into a tailspin of chaos and
despair, leaving the main characters dead in the end. It has been
said that one reason these stories are so wildly popular is that we as
humans can all relate to them. For within each of us lies a tragedy
of our own, the tragedy of grand-scheme disappointment. Sooner
or later we will all experience it. No one can avoid it altogether
in this life; it finds even the most loved, the most wealthy, the
most powerful people. Our common tragedy as people is one of
broken hope, unrealized dreams, and certain death- because of
our common sin.

BUT GOD.

GOD can make us better by burning off our dirt, cleansing us even as we suffer our greatest tragedies. *I am in awe of this!* This doesn't happen in Shakespeare's stories. But it <u>can</u> happen in mine and yours! Our tragedies don't *have* to end in death and despair! The transformation of our hearts from something hideous into something beautiful is a supernatural refining process. A *painful*, humbling process requiring much endurance, but one *worth* enduring- and one that only occurs when we choose to see Him in our suffering.

Seeing Christ in our suffering does not *remove* the suffering. It does not magically take away the travail of this life. But it gives us incredible strength to endure it, and to see value in it on a level that is beyond the physical realm. The tragedy I will describe in this chapter is one that used to be very hard for me to talk about. The colorful dreams I once dreamed with Mark in those middle-of-the-night talks and those walks through the woods, burned as bright hot flames for a long time. But over the years, those dream flames began to only flicker, sometimes very faintly, until they were extinguished almost entirely, by tragedy. But another kind of fire would be lit in me, one that would show me beautiful things about God-and ugly things about myself. I would undergo trial by holy fire. The fire that has been very hard to endure, but from which I am emerging more pure and more like Christ Jesus in my heart of hearts.

THE OTHER FAMILY MEMBER

In spring of 2008, just when things were beginning to be "on the mend" for our family, Mark began having back pain that was so severe, it was hard for him to walk. He was driving truck for a concrete company at the time. He had experienced back pain before, having been an avid adventurer and athlete in his youth. Mark was a football-playing, motorcycle riding, snow-machine jumping, karate-chopping, freight-hauling hunter and fisherman. He loved being active outdoors. He worked hard doing various physically demanding jobs. He liked to work and he took pride in work well done. Mark's back pain always subsided after a time of brief rest. But *this* time, it just kept growing worse no matter how much he tried to rest. This time *nothing* seemed to ease the pain, and the more he tried to work through it, the more attention it demanded. He had great difficulty climbing in and out of his truck and washing out the concrete barrel at the end of his shift. He would come home from work and just crawl into bed and try not to move until he had to get up the next morning. This continued awhile, until he just could not physically do it anymore. That was when our family's fifth member was born. Its name is PAIN.

When Pain moved in with us that spring, we had no idea how long it would stay. Pain crept in to our household stealthily. Quietly and gradually- subtle- like an assassin sneaking up for a kill. We did not notice the course of its destruction until we had been on it for awhile.

Mark took time off work to be evaluated medically for what was going on in his spine. There were few definitive answers, with little suggested remedy. Vertebral fracture was neither confirmed nor ruled out. Disc degeneration was evident in several of his vertebral discs, and the muscles and tendons of his middle and lower back were strained and inflamed. REST was the initial plan of treatment. So Mark rested. He really had no choice but to rest, as he could hardly move without pain. For a couple of months, he rested his back as much as he could.

But Pain did not pack his bags. It was here to stay awhile.

In those first months living with Pain, I went into "our love will carry us through anything" mode. I was *determined* not to be beaten down by this. I was content to serve Mark in any way I could, to ease his pain any way possible. I honestly thought that with enough love, prayer, and hope- and with positive habits of health and wellness- we could beat this thing and everything could just go back to normal soon. I was mistaken. It was going to take more than that, just to survive.

Pain showed itself to be a greedy fifth family member. Pain

was unrelenting. Demanding. Domineering. Selfish. Pain took away Mark's quality of life. He could no longer do the things he enjoyed. No more motorcycle riding. No more fishing or football tossing. Not even sitting up to play his saxophone. *Every*thing hurt. Mark could not enjoy a single thing. Even the simplest activities like driving, cooking, sitting on the couch to watch a movie, or taking a "quick" shower, proved too painful for Mark to endure. The only way he could be comfortable was lying down being still. Even then he was tormented with muscle spasms and tightness from which sleep was the only escape. In less than one year's time, Pain caused Mark to change from a confident, secure man of healthy mind and body to a bewildered, troubled person full of sorrow, fear, and anger. His confinement to the bed may as well have been to a small padded cell. The joys and aspirations of our life together were fading into a grey picture- a sloppy, frightening, distorted picture of nothing but that awful prison bed, pain pills, sleeping pills, and tears.

During the next three years, Mark's condition was evaluated by many doctors and specialists. Nutritionists, chiropractors, neurologists, physical therapists, orthopedic doctors, psychologists, pain management specialists- all had a hand in determining his prognosis. He was told his problems were due to multiple injuries sustained over time; that severe arthritis was now raging in the muscles of his middle and lower back, and there was nothing that could be done surgically to help him. His condition was permanent and could get worse, but was not likely to get better. The short-term and long-term forecasts were centered around just managing the pain and keeping his musculoskeletal system as healthy as possible. There was no talk of healing or how to get better. There was only a variety of suggested ways of learning how to cope, "how to live with it".

The decline of Mark's physical abilities and the relentlessness of his hurting led to the breakdown of his mental capacities. If you have ever tried to function with a severe backache, headache, earache, toothache, stomachache- you know how difficult it can be to accomplish anything productive as long as that pain is present. You just wait for it to "go away" so you can get back to your life. For Mark, the realization that this was probably never going to "go away"- that he may never "get his life back"- combined with the ongoing lack of accomplishments and inability to work and earn income- made him crazy. Quite literally crazy, at times. His pain, being impossible to "ignore", crippled him as much mentally as it did physically. Every activity became exponentially more difficult than it ought to be. Frustration became as regular as breathing to him. Discouragement became a way of life. He lost hope and began desiring death.

And so, he turned to whatever would take the edge off the pain. He self-medicated at times with alcohol, which easily lent itself to excess and brought with it its own gamut of strife and complications. He was on an ever-growing regimen of prescription narcotics, muscle relaxants, anti-depressants, and a sleeping aid. But incredibly, even with these around-the-clock meds, Pain remained with him, cold and heartless, jabbing him whenever he moved.

The side effects from the prescription drugs and from alcohol began to tear Mark apart from the inside out. His behavior became erratic, unpredictable, with extreme mood swings and uncontrolled emotions. Overdose was an ever-present threat, so much that I functioned in a state of constant alert, knowing that at any time Mark could overdose either accidentally or purposely. There were days I stayed home from work because I knew that leaving him alone would make suicide too easy. Mark was open with me about the temptation to end his own life.

I knew he was repeatedly asking God to take him.

I was repeatedly asking God to *heal* him.

All of this was happening to Mark. It was *his* trial by fire. But it was also happening to *me* and to our children. It is impossible for a father, a husband, to be tested so thoroughly without his family also being tested. And so, we were *all* in the fire together. We were *all* grieving the loss of what we once knew as a family.

Our old "better life" didn't exist anymore. With Pain now in our family portrait, everything was heading further and further away from perfect-- at dangerously high speeds-- and the brakes were giving out.

At times I would sit next to Mark on our bed- sometimes while he slept and other times while he was awake- placing my hand lightly over his back, pleading with God to keep him alive and to restore his physical body.

One night Mark awoke to a sharp, piercing pain in his chest, a frightening pain he had never felt before. It intensified when he inhaled air. I began to pray while dialing the phone for help. In the next moments, while speaking with an advice nurse, I was also speaking with God. My prayer was a begging sort of prayer.

"Please, God, *not tonight*! Spare his life, Lord! Don't take him now! I want him here with me! Please, Jesus, please *PLEASE* take this pain away!"

The advice nurse asked many questions, evaluating the nature of the problem, suggesting some things to try, and as we spoke and as I prayed, the pain came under control. It just started to subside. The nurse determined it was likely caused by a large bubble of trapped gas in Mark's upper abdomen. We were advised to "go get it checked out" in the emergency room. But Mark could feel it going away. And a trip to the emergency room was not an option in his mind at that time. "I'm OK, I really feel totally fine now," he said as he lied back down and fell quickly back into a peaceful sleep. But I remained there praying for a time. God answered my prayer that night. His steady hand calmed me through that experience, and I knew He was watching us and listening, even guiding that nurse to help us get through those moments which I thought might be Mark's last.

During those long months, Mark would often sleep for days at a time, waking only to use the restroom and to drink water. I hated this, but it was better than the alternatives of hearing him cry out in agony or hearing him speak of killing himself. His weeks of self-induced sedation were some of the hardest times our family walked through. I was torn between wanting him awake and wanting him at peace. I could not have both at the same time. Sleep was the only relief from the pain. Mark lost his appetite, his muscle strength, his desire for relationships, his vision for anything good in his future, his will to be alive.

Meanwhile, there was a household to run. When Pain moved in, our daughter Hannah was eight years old and our son Matthew was just six. I began working very hard to maintain a sense of normalcy in our home, not only for our children- but for all of us. The juggling act I had started back when Mark went trucking had gone from a level of "easy" to a level of "expert", as more and more balls were thrown at me, which I was expected to keep in the air continuously. I felt that if I let one of those balls fall, I would let somebody down, or things would begin to unravel for our family. So my daily energies were poured into helping Mark get through each day, getting him to and from doctor appointments, keeping our small apartment a nice place to live, teaching full time, balancing bills from month to month, and keeping meals on the table (which the Lord saw fit to do miraculously so many times, as I described previously). I encouraged our children to enjoy activities with friends and school groups as much as possible; the kids and I involved ourselves with church activities as much as we could. I had very little "me time", which I did not mind at first, but would grow to resent as time pressed on.

For Hannah and Matthew, "Daddy time" had changed from silly, active play - from being tossed around in the air and piggy-backing on his big strong shoulders, to lying quietly next to him to assemble a Lego structure or play a video game. We went from being outdoors often to almost never. Family drives were reduced from adventurous outdoor all-day excursions to stressful 20-minute trips for cheap ice cream or to a park where we could sit watching *other* kids having fun with *their* Daddies.

Those first years living with Pain were a roller coaster. Except, not the kind of roller coaster that's fun for its riders. It's the kind of roller coaster you can't get off, even though you want to- because you're scared and sick and you can't tell where is up or down anymore. You can't see the sky or the ground; everything is spinning. So you just close your eyes, wishing it could stop. You just hang on and hope it can end soon. That's what those years were like for our family.

THE FIRE THAT PURGES

What I did not fully understand then (but do now) is that God's hands were exposing me to an intense "fire" which would *purify me* from dirt I didn't even know I possessed.

God would prefer that none of us ever have to suffer. That was His intent from the beginning of time. It would have been that way, if not for sin. But because of the sin we are born with- our inheritance from Adam- a measure of suffering is brought upon us (sometimes a good measure of it). God allows this, knowing that our suffering has a way of getting rid of our dirt. He ultimately uses it for our good. Though, sometimes we can't see how that's possible- until we are on the other side of it.

Fire has had its own associations with God's revealing Himself to people. He has revealed His presence many times, through FIRE. His covenant with Abraham (Genesis 15:17). Moses standing at the burning bush (Exodus 3). The pillar of fire which led the Israelites in the wilderness at night (Exodus 13:21-22). Fires on altars that were continually burning. Sacrifices burnt to the God of Righteousness, the One without sin and without blemish. The flame tongues which appeared above the people's heads in the upper room, when Holy Spirit arrived on the day of Pentecost (Acts 2). These are just a few times God revealed Himself by fire. But the Bible also speaks of the fire in our lives--the refining process that is necessary *for the burning off of impurities.*

This figurative refining "fire" is *not* supposed to destroy us; its purpose is *not* to annihilate us, even though it might feel like that sometimes! "When you walk through the fire of oppression, you will not be burned up; the flames will not consume you." (Isaiah 43:2 TLB)

We are subjected to the refining fire in order to become *more pure.*

When gold is refined, it must be directly exposed to an intensely hot flame. This is not a gentle, mild heating; it is a drastic incineration! The gold is separated from any silver, iron, or other metals and minerals present in it. What remains after the burn is a more concentrated, pure gold. God says in Zechariah 13:9 (AMP), "I will bring (My people) through the fire, and will refine them as silver is refined and will test them as gold is tested. They will call on My name, and I will hear and answer them. I will say, It is My people; and they will say, The Lord is my God." *This is what has happened to me.* In enduring all the suffering caused by Mark's pain, I have called on God's name over and over again, often multiple times in a day or in an hour. He has heard my cry and He has answered. But His answer has <u>not</u> been, "I will take this all away right now and make it all better for you now- because you deserve it." He has not chosen to heal Mark in a miraculous instant. He has not removed Pain from the picture. Instead, His answers have caused me to see the filth in my own heart. They have required sacrifice. His answers have shown me that the fire is burning up a lot of garbage that I didn't even know was in my soul. (More about this in the next chapter.) I *don't* hate Him for that. I *thank* Him for it!

I have heard people say that God is a big old bully for putting us through the flame like He does. "How can God possibly have our best at heart while permitting us to endure such anguish in this life? How does that make any sense?" Well, it doesn't always-- *to us.* But if we zoom out to look at the big picture of our lives, if we analyze it honestly through the lens of Scripture and with the mind of Christ, we can see how many parts of us are actually strengthened because of our enduring that fire. Maybe our faith is being increased. Maybe our character or our physical body is being strengthened. Maybe a growth is taking place- a growth in confidence, determination, wisdom, or tenacity. Maybe a higher love is being achieved! But I dare say in *all* cases, the fire that purges is *cleaning up our dirty hearts.* Just like closets and file cabinets, refrigerators, and dumpsters must be purged of the junk they accumulate, our *hearts* must also be de-junked! Pretty often. And pretty aggressively at times.

For me, God's refining fire has helped me see my own flawed motivations, my selfishness and apathy, my deep-rooted lust for everything *I* want instead of what *others* need. If I had never endured suffering...if Pain had never come to live with us... I would not have shared closely in Christ's suffering. I would not know His self-sacrifice so deeply. *How can we really understand what He endured for us if we never endure anything?* Because of the fire that purges, my love for Jesus and for others has intensified. I associate better with others suffering around me. *How can we understand another person's pain if we never experience our own?* The members of Christ's body (you and I!) should have a mutual interest in each other and care for one another. If one part suffers, all the parts share the suffering. (I Corinthians 12:25-26) *This sharing in one another's sufferings is done more readily as we relate to one another's painful experiences.*

EMERGING FROM THE FIRE

I have no doubt you have suffered in your own life. What has been *your* great tragedy? What higher purpose might God have in mind for you *in* your tragedy? Has it drawn you closer to Him? Could it be that He is using your suffering to *strengthen* you somehow, in your soul and spirit? Has it cleaned you up in some way? Maybe you are in the fire right now. Maybe you are wondering *why* God would allow such pain in your life. Talk to God about that! Ask Him to show you what impurities- what junk- your own refinement process is burning off. He will show you!

The God of heaven has shown me over and over, in His Word and in my prayer and worship times and through the testimony of others, that *our purpose in suffering is not to wallow around in it and try to find a way out of it.* Our purpose is not to make excuses or to feel continually sorry for ourselves. *Our purpose in suffering is to see Christ's suffering, to know it firsthand, to experience it more deeply so we can love Him and other people with a love that is more perfect, more like <u>His</u> love!* And we will experience His hand helping us through it, holding us right through the moments of agony. And we will see how He helped us get through it. I Peter 4:13 tells us that as we share in His suffering, we can actually rejoice, knowing that when His radiant glory is finally revealed to the world, our triumph will be greater, more exultant. Knowing that our suffering is truly FINALLY over- because of JESUS- will make the whole experience of heaven that much more magnificent. I dream about that day more than anything else now!

God isn't bullying us by allowing the fire to have its place in our lives. He sees the heightened beauty- the righteousness- which will shine through us when we emerge victorious out of it! God *will* bring us through the fire. He will do it in His good time. He already has started bringing us through it! He will say of us, *"They will come with weeping, pouring out prayers for the future--and I will cause them to walk by streams of water and bring them in a straight way in which they will not stumble. Their life shall be like a watered garden, and they shall not sorrow or languish any more at all. I will turn their mourning into joy and will comfort them. And My people will be satisfied with my goodness." (Jeremiah 31:9-14 AMP)*

And when we walk out of our purifying fire, we will be more than alright. We will be bearers of His righteousness, testifiers of His goodness, proclaiming to Him, *"We went through fire, but You brought us out into a broad, moist place- to abundance and refreshment and the open air!" Psalm 66:12 (AMP)*

CHAPTER 15

HOLY HANDS

*"And I shall turn mind hand to thee, and seethe out thy
filth, until thou be cleansed." Isaiah 1:25 (WYC)*

On Easter Sunday 2010, two years after Pain moved in, we
attempted attending church as a family. Half-way into the worship
time, I looked over at Mark to see him clenching the seat in front of
him, sweating profusely, looking pale and forcing a half-smile that
was trying to look happy but was not fooling me. He was tolerating
excruciating pain.

"Look at him trying so hard", I thought. "That's my courageous
Mark."

I was so proud of him for making the effort. I knew he was
doing it mostly for me and the kids. But I also knew there was a
good chance he'd pass out before the end of the service. He lasted
about 40 minutes, just part-way into the message, before making
the difficult walk back to the truck. The drive home was silent
except for the cries and sighs of defeat coming from Mark's depths,
and the quiet weeping coming from *my* depths. It was a mournful

day, one I don't like to think about. We all knew Daddy could not go to church again for awhile. By the time he got up the stairs back into our apartment and back to bed, I was so emotionally exhausted that I just sat and stared at a wall for awhile. Too numb to do anything else, and too broken-hearted even to pray. *Happy Easter, everyone.*

Up until that point, I had done pretty well not asking God, "Why?" But now I began to ask Him.

"Why, God? Why would you allow this? *Why* would You take away Mark's livelihood? *How could You* let him deteriorate like this? *Why* can't we even go to church together as a family? Don't You want that for us? Do You really care about us at *all*? We're supposed to be missionaries for You, God! Don't You want that? *How could You do this to us?"*

What was sprouting in my spirit was a harsh resentment that would grow into huge thorny weeds which God would need to pull with His own hands. I resented Mark's pain. I resented Mark for his *responses* to the pain. Mark grew increasingly angry about his circumstance, angry that we couldn't get ahead financially, angry that he hurt all the time. That anger manifested often, in fits of fury, and I seemed to have a way of stepping right in its path. There were times when Mark made selfish choices and said hurtful things in condescending tones. There were times when he was up in the night, frantic with pain, raging out of control and, consequentially, out of his mind. Times when he would lash out verbally at me and the kids. Times when he was so absorbed in his own hurts that he could not see ours. I resented that.

I resented God for allowing Pain to scourge the man I loved.

I resented God for not healing him yet.

"Where are You, God? Why this cruel injustice?"

The more I demanded answers from God, the more upset I grew when I did not get them. The more I expressed my feelings of injustice to Him, the more unjust I perceived Him to be. I stopped accepting that things were so hard in our home. The more I resented God, the more I resented Mark. The more I resented

Mark, the less I wanted to be near him. I began desiring some *other* life, in some other place, *away* from Mark, away from Pain, away from all the "drama" those two could conjure up together.

Deadly Daydreams

I daydreamed too much about this other fantasy life. It was one I could escape to in my mind, one without all the heartache and problems of my real life. It was a life in which I was appreciated and cherished, a life that treated me with respect and gratitude. It was a life with romance, with laughter, with adventure and fun (all of which, I felt, were severely lacking in the hand I had been dealt). Ironically, this "alternate reality" I got lost in mentally was also full of effective ministry (imaginary ministry) to other people. I thought, "I could do so much more for Jesus if I were single again! If I could be free of Mark, then I could finally go be a missionary! I could do more at church if I wasn't 'tied down' like this at home!" I actually believed my intentions were good. Though my intentions for ministry had been good at one time, deep down they were not good anymore; for they were deep-rooted in self-gratifying desire rather than a genuine seeking out of what God wanted my life to be about. A long list began forming in my mind, of things in life that would just be easier and better if I could somehow break free of Mark and Pain. (Now I see that list was a lie I listened to; but at the time, it seemed like undeniable truth.) I was convinced that if my marriage ended, so would this misery in which I found myself.

Slowly and without realizing what was really happening, my daily ambitions became more about me and less about anyone else. In my heart, I wanted that other life- and the daydream became more like an unwritten mission statement in my soul. As the bud of resentment sprouted up in my will, it bloomed into full-on selfishness. And I began to regularly utter three words in my spirit and soul, words that often lead to nowhere good:

"*What about __me__?*"

While the world says it's OK to live life asking and answering that question, God would show me the hard way that my life wasn't just about me, no matter how much I thought it should be.

"But it's my life! Shouldn't it be about ME?!?"

God's answer, quite opposite from the world's, always came swiftly: *"No."*

I did not want to hear His answer. Hearing that my life is not about me is *still* hard to hear, hard to accept. And I think it will be, for as long as sin is in the picture.

I wanted to run away from my reality. I wanted to get away from Mark's tears and the dark negativity that pervaded our home and our future together. "I don't deserve this," I told myself. "I didn't sign up for this! I am entitled to more than this pathetic existence! If I wanted to be a "single" Mom, I would have lived in promiscuity! If I wanted to be a round-the-clock caregiver, I'd run a nursing home! This is *not* what I want for my life! There is no fun here, no romance, no freedom. I can't do what *I* want to do! I can't believe this is my life! What about *my* dreams? What about what *I* want?!?"

That self-centered question (and the self-centered daydream answer I was choosing) threatened the life of my marriage in a big way. It threatened the spiritual security of my children. Not to mention the spiritual well-being of the man I was contemplating leaving. You see, my enemy Satan wanted my marriage dead. He wanted to kill what was left of God's love in me. And I was letting him do it, just by entertaining notions of another life I wished I had.

THE SLOW FADE

Self-pride was overtaking me, but slowly- so that I hardly noticed it happening. I was allowing my love for myself to surpass my love for God and others, especially for Mark.

At the root of every sin is self-pride. Selfish pride was there when Lucifer challenged God. It was there in the garden of Eden when Eve and Adam took of the fruit. It is there in *every choice* we make that is based on a fleshly desire. I went from loving Mark with the passionate pursuit I described previously-- wanting to always be with him-- to despising him, wanting to get away from him. Through a series of letdowns, hurts, and disappointments, I found that I could stop loving Mark-and even start hating him-and somehow it seemed justified. But God would make it clear to me that it *wasn't* justifiable at all.

One afternoon He did this while I was driving home alone in my car. It happened almost exactly a year after the Easter Sunday letdown. (I had been asking God "Why?" and "What about me?" for a year.)

Listening to Christian radio that day in the car, a song played that I had not heard before. Its words grabbed hold of me so tight, made me cry so hard that I had to pull the car over. The words described the progressive destruction that comes when we choose to give in to temptation and sin, a little bit at a time, until our lives begin to crumble apart. The song spoke of the high price of willful wrongdoing, the hard consequences of poor choices. "*The journey from your mind to your hands is shorter than you're thinking,*" warned the song. And as I listened with my ears and my heart, I heard God's voice telling me very clearly, "Davida, *this* is what is happening to you. You are slowly fading out of My favor and into an existence ruled by your flesh. You are giving your heart away to your flesh, Davida, when you are supposed to be *killing* your flesh. You have forgotten that your heart belongs to *Me*."

I could not disagree with Him at all. He was right. I had "given Him my heart" long ago, but I kept taking it back because I was so unhappy with how my life was going. The radio song was describing a crumbling happening in *my* heart, in *my* marriage, in our family unit. The song was *Slow Fade* by Casting Crowns,[1] and the words that grasped me the tightest were these: *Families never crumble in a day. It's a slow fade.*

It had happened over time. My marriage to Mark was collapsing, and it would fall flat if we didn't turn things around.

I know it was no accident that I heard that song that day in the car. In that encounter, God unveiled the overall picture of our *spiritual battle*, the battle that was being fought through Mark's back pain, through our ever-dwindling finances, our poor health, our broken dreams, everything. I knew our evil enemies were fighting against us, and I saw- for the first time- how *I was letting them win*. He also unveiled His plan for my fight. I knew I had to fight my enemies off with a purer love, with a sacrifice. *A sacrifice of my own desires.* Right there in the car, while still pulled over, the music still playing, I knew I had to choose love for Mark and for my children <u>over what I wanted for myself</u> if our family unit was to be preserved. I knew that choice was possible, because Jesus made that choice when He endured the cross. I knew that the power of Christ's love was big enough to reverse the disdain I had in my heart, this fading that was going on in the depths of my being. But giving up what *I* wanted? Well, that HURT. It hurt a lot. It was the hardest thing I had ever done up to that point. It meant giving up some stuff I had desired for a long time.

"*Is this what it was like for You on the cross, Lord? Is this something like what it took for You to hang there in bloody pain, for all of us?"*

In those moments I envisioned Jesus up on His cross of pain, and I came into a higher understanding of the level of sacrifice He had made for me there. Jesus had endured *far* worse than I was being asked to endure, for my sake. Couldn't I endure *this* for *His*? I asked Him to help me see the black and white again, the clarity of His Word, to help me make good choices that would please Him.

He <u>did</u> help me. But I still cried for a week. Gut-wrenching crying that lasts an hour or two and leaves you completely wrung out afterward. A wrestling match was going on in my insides: the decision to please God or to please myself. But my soul was resounding the truth of Proverbs 11:2 (AMP): *"When swelling and pride come, then emptiness and shame come also. But with the humble (those who are lowly, who have been pruned or chiseled by trial, and <u>renounce self</u>) are skillful and Godly wisdom and soundness."*

HIS HOLINESS MY HOLINESS

I cried many tearful prayers that week. But mostly, it was because I was giving up the daydreams, the longings for something else besides what the Lord had already given me. Like a child in a store, holding a desired toy, and crying when told, "No, you can't have that now." I sat on our living room couch that weekend, hour after hour, studying various passages- gathering ammunition that would help me combat the devil who I knew was at work against me. And these words of God continually lingered in my mind:

"**BE *HOLY*, for I am holy.**"

These words from Leviticus 11:44 (AMP) were spoken by God when He was giving the Israelites specific instructions for the diet they were to have. His whole reason for the restricted diet was that His people would be set apart from every other people group in that day. His people would be sanctified; they would be *different*. Different from everybody else. That's one way the world would know they were *His* people; that they were special--that they belonged to Him. "I have brought you out of your captivity, out of your bondage," the Lord told them. "I have brought you out to be your God. So be holy, for I am holy!" He was telling them, "You will be different from everyone else, as I am different! You will be set apart!" I imagine it was really hard for many of those Israelites to give up the foods He was asking them to give up. I imagine that not all of them really *wanted* to be different. That's where obedience would come in.

That weekend on the couch, I knew the Lord was calling me to obey Him, *to stay in my reality*, to face it head-on with all of its challenges, to stop wishing it away, and to purify my heart so that I could do all of that the right way. I did a study on purity in the Bible, which led me to scores of passages about the holiness of God. I was blown away, seeing His holiness more clearly than I ever had before.

The word "holy" actually means SET APART-- *DIFFERENT* from everyone else. What sets God apart from all of us is that HE IS COMPLETELY SINLESS. Christ lived as a man on this Earth, but His COMPLETE SINLESSNESS sets Him apart. And although we cannot become completely sinless in this life, we *can* live this life as unto Christ, striving to live as He lived, which means eschewing sin, pushing sin away, literally running away from it when we need to! It means choosing what is right, according to God's Word. Doing the next right thing, one decision at a time. We can live this life in an attitude of rebellion, ignoring our tendencies for sin. Or we can see our sins for what they are, directly and purposely turning away from them- as many times as we have to in a week, a day, an *hour*. To refuse repentance by knowingly sinning with our minds and bodies is to defile the very temple of God Who dwells in us. "Don't you know that you are God's temple and that God's Spirit dwells in you? Anyone destroying God's temple will be destroyed. For God's temple is holy. And *you* are that temple!" (I Corinthians 3: 16-17)

Those hours on the couch, I talked with the Lord about this

call to holiness. "How is *my life* going to be set apart? How is it going to be *holy*?" I asked.

"You're not going to abandon Mark," He answered. "You're going to get back to <u>real</u> love, *My* love, and you're going to stop putting yourself before your family. You're going to be a faithful bride, in heart and body, and keep the covenant promise you made- to the higher love I have called you to! This higher love is what will show the world that you are Mine! This is what will set you apart. Let *My* holiness be *your* holiness!"

My teary eyes were un-blindfolded again, opened widely to see the correlation between unfaithfulness in a marriage and unfaithfulness to Jesus. Just as Judas betrayed Jesus and Peter denied Him on the night of His arrest, I was betraying and denying my husband in my heart- and in so doing, I was betraying Jesus, too. I was rationalizing this by telling myself I deserved "a better marriage", a "better" love. But I knew Jesus wanted me to honor my promise to Mark. It didn't matter what Mark had done (or not done). No one else's actions would ever give <u>me</u> a free license to sin. Nothing would justify my heart of unfaithfulness. Sin is sin, and I saw mine for what it was, so different from what Jesus' unfailing devotion to me looked like.

"Jesus would not abandon me the way I am abandoning my husband. No matter how I hurt Jesus, He will keep loving me! He didn't make excuses on the cross. He didn't back out of His promise to me. And no matter how badly and frequently I let Him down, He always takes me back." *Wow.* His humility was pouring into me, changing me.

How could I break Jesus' heart with these thoughts I was having? How could I hurt Him by hurting Mark and my family?

I couldn't.

That was the point when my love for Jesus and others was widened. The point when my love for Him surpassed my love for self, resulting in a greater love for others. It was the point when the ugly weeds of infidelity and self-pride were pulled at their roots by holy hands.

HIGHER LOVE

Around the same time, I was challenged to take the words of I Corinthians 13 (the famous "love chapter" of the Bible) and replace the word "love" with my name, in verses 4-7. It was a self-reflection to see how true the statements would be if they were to be said about me. It was pretty eye-opening.

"Davida is patient; Davida is kind." *Ya, OK, that's pretty true....* "Davida is not proud, not self-seeking, not easily angered." *Um, well.... no... not exactly...*

"Davida keeps no record of wrongs." *Uh-oh. Not so at all...* "Davida always hopes, always perseveres." *Wow. No. I hardly do those things at all anymore. I just want to throw in the towel and run away.*

God used this instance to show me that the "love" I *thought* I was full of, for Mark especially (but for others too) was not pure as it should have been. Did I really love people the way I pretended to? In my heart, I knew I didn't. My love fell far short from what it would be if I were *truly* like Christ. In those roughest times of my marriage, the times I was hurt and disappointed by my earthly husband, I saw the perfection of my heavenly Groom, Jesus, MORE brightly. I saw how much higher and purer His love is than the love that Mark and I were demonstrating toward each other at that time. I saw how beautiful Jesus' self-sacrifice was, how much He deserved *my* sacrificial love.

If I had not been through that experience, I could not sing about "the beauty of His holiness" with as much conviction as I can now. I see Him more clearly because of His holy fire. I appreciate Him more. I love my husband better. I love my children better. I love everybody better.

A miracle in the midst of tragedy.

Has God been prompting you to abandon a particular sin or an attitude of rebellion? Has He been showing you His purity, calling *you* to a higher love? Can you see the beauty of His holiness? How might *your* life be set apart as holy before a sinless, loving Savior?

I encourage you to get alone with Jesus somewhere and study the words "purity" and "holiness" in His Word. Purposely *look to see* His perfection. He will show you His holy hands! And He will cleanse your own hands to be clean like His.

"Who is like You, O Lord?
Who is like You, glorious in holiness, awesome
in splendor, working wonders?

You stretched out your hand,
(and) in Your loving-kindness have led forth
the people whom You have redeemed.
You have guided them in Your strength to Your holy habitation."
Exodus 15:11-13 (AMP)

CHAPTER 16

THE ARMS OF FORGIVENESS

*"Indeed, what I have forgiven has been for your sake in
the presence of Christ, so that we would not be outwitted
by Satan; for we are not ignorant of his designs."*
II Corinthians 2:10-11 (ESV)

You know that feeling when you've gone and blown it and you
know you hurt somebody, and you wish you could undo it, but you
know you never can? I know that feeling well. I think we all do. It's
one that can eat us up inside- quickly in an instant, or slowly over
a long stretch of time. The feeling can be torturous. It can make
us lose sleep, lose appetite, lose faith in ourselves. It's damaging.

If you are a human being reading this, you've been on the
other side of that feeling too. You've been the one hurt, the one
standing there dumbfounded, wondering, "What just happened?"
after someone just hurt you in the core of your being, maybe so
badly that you feel you are beyond repair.

Neither side of that feeling is a good place to be standing. Both
are dismaying. If only our offenses could be undone the moment

we realize their ruinous harm. If only an offender could just say, "Oops, I messed up; please forgive me" and the person he offended could just say, "OK, I forgive you" and that would be it-- case closed, no more pain or sorrow from the incident. But not so. We all know it is a lot more complicated than that. Forgiveness is not something that comes easily. It's often accompanied with some amount of teeth-gnashing, blood, sweat, and tears. Forgiveness rubs against our desire for justice, our need for validation, our wish to be in the right.

The fact of the matter is, we all hurt people and we are all hurt *by* people. No one has hurt no one, and no one will be hurt by no one. And so, we ALL are walking around with chains, bound in spirit and soul to the people we have hurt and who have hurt us. We have been wounded in our souls, and at the same time we carry guilt (sometimes immense) from our mistakes, from wounds we have inflicted on others. So often, the ones who wrong us the most frequently and deeply are the ones we love the most, the ones we spend the most time with. In parent-child and sibling relationships, this hurt and guilt can become so heavy a strain that it wears the relationship down to a nub- and can destroy it completely before long. The same thing happens in husband-wife relationships. Separation and divorce are ugly consequences of hurts inflicted by one or both spouses on one or both spouses, with no resolution---often because forgiveness does not come easily.

Our great enemy Satan uses this cycle of hurt, guilt, and unforgiveness to destroy us. He cunningly uses the hurt of a sin offense to bring down both the offender *AND* the offended one. Satan *hates* forgiveness. It undoes his guile.

The night I learned true forgiveness was a night I will never forget. It happened one evening while walking my dog...

The nightly chore was sometimes a real bummer. I didn't even *want* to get a dog in the first place, and here I was stuck doing the last walk of the day, every day. Ugh! But cute little Daisy was growing on me, and so was the walking. Well, sort of. Some nights I really minded it- like those cold, rainy nights when I was tired or didn't feel well, or my feet hurt or I just wasn't in the mood. On those nights, the last thing I felt like doing was walking the little mutt down a flight of stairs, around the apartment complex- only to scoop her doggie doo into a plastic bag and dispose of it in the creepy community dumpster before walking back up the flight of stairs to our apartment. But *some* nights, the walk was a welcome break from the apartment. A time to listen to music, or to think and pray, or just to take a break from noise and thinking, just to breathe in the quiet, moist night air. Sometimes I took an extra long time on the walk. Sometimes that walk was the only (much-needed) time I had to myself. This was one of those nights.

The moonlight was not bright this particular night, but the sky was clear and the air was crisp and cool. As I headed down the damp, dirty stairway and made the left turn to walk down the sidewalk that ran along our building, my feet could not carry me fast enough. My pace notably quicker than usual, I felt like I could continue walking all night. But my faster pace and desire to keep walking were not because of a happy heart or an intent for a good cardio workout. It was anger. It seemed each footstep was driven by anger that had been building in me all day long. I could have exploded with it. But I was holding back. It was bottled up but ferociously teeming, bubbling up in me- rather violently. I probably pulled on poor Daisy's leash a little too hard a few times, as she liked to pull off to the side sometimes. That night I wasn't sure how I could go back to the apartment. I was that mad. I decided I'd better just walk around long enough to cool down. I needed to calm the volcano that was trying to erupt in me.

What had occurred that day was a series of separate but connected incidents of hurt. It was a bad day for Mark, one of those angry days when Pain got the better of him more than once. I couldn't do or say the right things, and the more I tried, the more I aggravated him, and I just didn't know how to be anymore. With verbal insults, thoughtless remarks, and disapproving glances, Mark had caused some emotional harm to me that day. *I was not OK.* My soul was bleeding from the repeated stabs it had sustained over the course of the day. And what was worse, our children had witnessed several of these incidents of hurt. They could see exactly what was going on. I was infuriated by this. I'd held my anger in check most of the day, but now it wanted to be unleashed.

The problem for my anger (and for my enemy Satan) was that I had been to church earlier that same evening, where I had listened to a message about forgiveness. The message, brought by my dear friend who had <u>no</u> idea what I was going through that day, was simple and clear. It was like no talk on forgiveness I had ever heard before. Because I couldn't get it out of my head. I'd seen illustrations that night which made me view forgiveness in a new light- as *my choice*- a choice that could lead to freedom. The revelation I received that night at church- about forgiveness- was now competing with self-pride and anger for dominance in my mind. And that was making me *MORE* angry! I didn't WANT to think about forgiveness right now. I didn't WANT to forgive Mark! I'd had enough of that.

I wanted vengeance.

The Bondage of Unforgiveness

When someone hurts you emotionally, you become shackled immediately by that hurt. The person who committed the offense against you also becomes shackled, by his conscience. Knowing he has wronged you, he feels guilty about the offense. The wrongful act connects the two of you. Whether your offender is a stranger, someone you hardly know, or someone you deeply love, you are bound together by the offense.

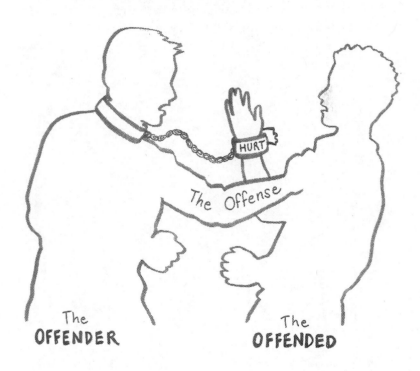

THE GRUDGE OF UNFORGIVENESS

Your offender and you remain bound together emotionally AND spiritually, by unforgiveness. A grudge forms in you, against your offender. The hurt that you feel is continually transferred into the grudge you have against that person, sustaining the bond between you. No matter how much distance is put between you and your offender, this bondage will remain until forgiveness takes place. The offender should ask for forgiveness, but he may never do so. It is up to you, the offended one, to initiate the forgiveness-- to initiate the liberation of yourself from your offender.

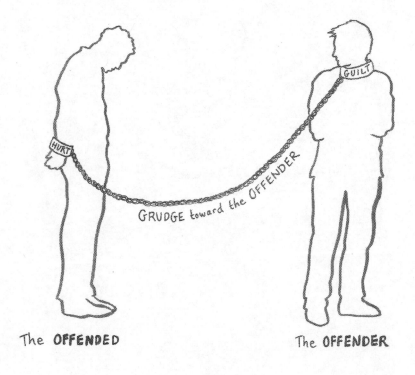

The **OFFENDED**   The **OFFENDER**

THE FORGIVENESS ACT

YOU can REMOVE your offender's guilt, whether he requests this or not. You do this by choosing to stop blaming your offender for what he did to you. By choosing to stop dwelling on it. By giving up the grudge you have against him.

This is forgiveness. It is an *action*.

The
OFFENDED   The
OFFENDER

PLACING IT ALL IN BIGGER HANDS

Then you give the hurt, the grudge, the offense itself, and your offender TO GOD. (Another *action!*) You place these all in the hands of God. *Vengeance is left to God.* He will deal with your offender from now on. You are free of the offense now. Free of the hurt, free of the grudge. Free to accept the healing Jesus will bring to your soul. Free to walk in this new freedom and be unshackled-- forever!

The **OFFENDED**

True forgiveness frees the offended one who has chosen to perform its action. True forgiveness may not seem "fair". It wasn't "fair" that you got hurt in the first place. God didn't hurt you. SIN did that. Sin hurts and destroys. Forgiveness *repairs.* Forgiving the person who wronged you brings healing to your soul. A healed soul is a free soul. *It is worth the effort!* The action of forgiveness may need to be repeated again and again- for the same offense- as we tend to put those shackles back on. We take the grudge back. *God wants us to leave it with Him for good.*

That night on my walk with Daisy, I wasn't sure forgiveness *was* worth the effort.

As I neared the large open patch of grass at the edge of our apartment complex, I began to sob. I cried out to God in my bitter brokenness.

"How can this be right, God? How can I *possibly* forgive Mark? I can't, God! *I can't this time!* I'm so done! Enough already with the forgiveness, God! I don't want to do it anymore. It's not fair."

I carried on like this for a few moments, before stopping on a little hill near the roadside. Watching all the cars race past the apartment complex, I wanted to be in one of them. *Couldn't someone come and take me out of here? Take me away from this so I wouldn't have to face Mark again?*

Still crying and rejecting the message I had heard just a few hours ago, I looked around and felt like everything stopped for a minute. It was as though someone had hit a "pause" button on the running movie of my life. Everything went quiet in that moment-except for the words, "Forgive him. Forgive him as many times as you have to."

People talk about the "still small voice" of the Lord's Spirit. This voice was still, but small it was <u>not</u>. It was big. It shook me up. It was booming like fireworks in the sky. I kept hearing it repeat again and again. "Forgive as many times as you have to!" *Well, how many times am I going to have to?*

"As many times as I have forgiven *you*. Remember, seventy times seven!"

Then, there on the hill- with the dog sniffing around on the ground next to me, the cars whizzing by on that dark cool night- I remembered how Peter had asked Jesus the very same question. "How many times must I forgive my offender, Jesus?" and Jesus replied, "Seventy times seven times!" This was a symbolic way of saying, "*Infinite* number of times. AS MANY TIMES AS YOU HAVE TO."

There in the grass, I had vivid images of Jesus carrying His cross. The sky may as well have been lit up with images of Jesus walking up to Golgotha, the Place of the Skull, beaten and bleeding- yet to suffer the worst of it. I could see Him dying; I could hear His words in my head..."Father, forgive them. They don't know what they are doing!" And hearing that, I began to calm down. My crying turned from an angry cry to a humbled cry; I could feel anger beginning to leave me. I was seeing Jesus' forgiveness in a way I had not before. He was showing me the depth of it, the pain of it, the necessity of it.

"Jesus, *how* did You do that? How did You forgive those people for hurting You so badly?"

He did that because He was Love incarnate. He was Pardon in the flesh. He had been born of Mary for a specific purpose, for the forgiveness of sins. Forgiveness was His mission. It was His ministry. Jesus Christ was the divine embodiment of forgiveness.

"I'm not like You, Jesus. I just don't have it in me! I'd like to, but I don't."

He struck that thought down so quickly; I knew I was being rebuked in my spirit.

"You have *My* power in you. I am alive in you! I have given you all authority to forgive *the same way I do*, by the power of the Spirit of the Living God! So do it, Davida! Do it *NOW*! Come into My healing!"

He also reminded me of my own hypocrisy. *How could I expect God to forgive me when I wouldn't forgive someone else?* Jesus told a story about that once. The parable of the unmerciful servant. He was pretty clear about what could happen to someone who refuses to forgive while expecting the Lord to forgive him. It isn't pretty. (Matthew 18:21-35)

If I were to paint a scene of those moments- hashing it out with God - the painting would show me there on the grass; with large letters glowing brightly like skywriting in the black night sky above my head, twinkling and bursting like sparklers on the 4th of July. The writing, illuminated so splendidly that there's NO way it could be missed, spells, "*FORGIVE!*"

Jesus revealed Himself as my Forgiver so that I would forgive Mark. As many times as I had to. And so I *did* forgive him that night. I walked back to the apartment, *a changed soul.* Another encounter with God had occurred. In an unexpected and undeniable way, the Lord God had shown me the beauty of His forgiving arms. I ran to them, just as the prodigal son ran to his father's arms (Luke 15:20). I was met with a fervent embrace, a holy kiss, a celebration. It felt good to obey. It felt good to please the Father. It felt right because it *was* right.

When we choose what is right in God's eyes over what is right in our own sight, He opens our eyes to see more of people's pain-and this helps us to be better forgivers.

God helped me see the struggles Mark was enduring, and that made it easier to forgive him. I believe forgiveness- not just on my part, but on Mark's part as well- has spared our marriage from death. Forgiving my spouse has made it easier for me to forgive *others* in my life who've wronged me. Although I still must choose forgiveness multiple times- sometimes in a day or hour- the more I choose it, the more easily that choice comes the next time. *It's possible to become a habitual forgiver!!*

The world doesn't value forgiveness the way that God does. The world will not understand a choice to forgive, to love, in spite of being wronged. Jesus acknowledged this when He said, "You have heard that it was said, 'An eye for an eye and a tooth for a tooth!' But I say to you...if anyone slaps you on the right cheek, turn to him the other also....And if anyone forces you to go one mile, go with him *two* miles!" (Matthew 5:38-41 ESV) People around you who observing your forgiveness will pay attention. They may question your decision. They may ask, *"How* can you let that go? How can you forgive *that?"* This is a way you can show Jesus to them! It is a way you can testify of *HIS* forgiveness! It is a way you will be **set apart** in front of the world. (This relates back to the holiness discussed in the last chapter!) *The world will notice authentic forgiveness.* It stands out because it is special. It is achieved in Christ!

If you can think back on a time in your life when someone else forgave you, consider how that released you from guilt that had been laid upon your soul. Then think also about Jesus on His cross. Reflect on all the times He's forgiven you, all the sins you've committed against Him, that HE HAS FORGIVEN. *Jesus is best at removing guilt from a heart of regret!* Follow His example! He has removed your sin and it is remembered no more. As you strive to see Him and be like Him, He *will* help you forgive others! You will walk in His freedom. You will stand in His arms of forgiveness.

"He (the Lord) never bears a grudge, nor remains angry forever. He has not punished us as we deserve for all our sins, for His mercy toward those who fear and honor Him is as great as the height of the heavens above the earth. He has removed our sins as far away from us as the east is from the west." Psalm 103:9-12 (Living Bible)

A Note About Abuse

I feel it is important to clarify that forgiveness must not be confused with tolerating *abuse*. If you are in some type of relationship in which you are repeatedly hurt, and your offender demonstrates no intent to *stop* hurting you, it may be necessary for you to withdraw physically and emotionally from that person who is causing you harm. Still forgive that person, yes- certainly. Forgive again and again. But seek Godly counsel to help you in your circumstance. Talk to Jesus- and to others who know Him- about your situation. Get advice from a person who has demonstrated forgiveness, but who also understands boundary-setting.

If you are in a place of real danger to your body, spirit, and soul-- it may be time to get away from that place, at least for a time but maybe permanently- in order for healing to come to you. *Do not bear abuse alone.* Satan will use your abuse mightily against you, in an attempt to bring you down spiritually. Place yourself on a supportive platform with people who will help you make decisions that are best for you.

You can set healthy boundaries without harboring unforgiveness in your heart.

Act carefully and wisely, and pray continuously.

The Lord will guide you to safety in His perfect way.

CHAPTER 17

GLOWING HANDS THAT HEAL ME

*"While Jesus was in one of the towns, there came a man covered
with leprosy. When he saw Jesus, he fell on his face and implored
Him, saying, 'Lord, if You are willing, cure me and make me
clean.' And Jesus reached out His hand and touched him, saying,
'I am willing; be cleansed!' And immediately the leprosy left him."*
Luke 5:12-13 (AMP)

Only recently have I come to understand that I am a person in
three parts, just as God is in three parts. I've also come to know
that healing isn't just needed in *one* part of me. It's needed in *all
three* parts. Body. Soul. Spirit.

At age 15 I found myself the sickest I've ever been in my life. I
was in Mexico when a tiny arthropod decided to help itself to some
part of my flesh, and in so doing, injected an illness called typhus
into my circulatory system. It didn't take long for typhus (what
used to be called "typhoid fever") to fully manifest itself. Fainting
spells, delirium-induced hallucinations, fever, chills, diarrhea,
pain, vomiting. If I had been living a century earlier, I might not
have survived it. But thanks to God and the wonders of modern

medicine, I got better. I missed three weeks of the 10th grade and it took me months to get back to full bodily health. Although it was getting most of the attention at the time, my body was not the only part of me that needed healing. If I had understood this back then, I may have been spared pain in those coming-of-age years.

The body is the "suit" worn by the soul and spirit. All of us are well aware of the body we've been given- as well as its limitations. We cannot make our bodies do whatever we want them to do. They are limited by the laws of physics, by the capacities of the very cells that constitute them. I can't make myself grow taller or shrink or disappear. My body won't let me.

The soul is limited too. I've experienced more freedom of soul than I ever have in body, but I am still well aware of my soul's limitations. Your soul is your mind, will, and emotions. It is what you think about, what you desire, what you *feel*. It is your heart. It is the depths of yourself and the part that others won't usually see unless you allow them to. It is much more secret than the body, and it can limit you just as your body can. Your soul has a certain vulnerability that can work against you if you're not careful. Self-control and self-monitoring are required for soul care, just as for body care.

Then there's the part of you that isn't body or soul. Your spirit. Your spirit is the part of you that you are least likely to know. You probably know your own body quite well, you may know your soul very well (although lots of people seem very confused about their own souls). But who gets to know their spirit? What is the spirit anyway?

Spirit is that part of you that connects you to God your Maker. Your spirit lasts forever; it is not destructible in the same way your body and mind are. Your spirit outlasts your body and soul; it remains when the other two fade. Your spirit won't ever stop existing. It will live for all eternity- either in peace with Jesus or in torment without Him.

For all of my youth and early adulthood, I knew I was more than a body. I thought I was comprised of body and spirit, and that my spirit was the same thing as my soul. Not so. Now I know.

Why am I telling you all this? How does this relate to revelation and healing?

Well-- most people, when thinking about "healing", think about PHYSICAL healing. And certainly, the physical body has frequent need for healing. But "healing" does not apply only to your body! Your soul and spirit need healing too! They are two different things, *connected* to your body. The three comprise a three-part cord that makes you YOU. What makes YOU unique ("you-nique!") is that *no one else has the exact same combination of strands making the cord that is your being.* All three strands were created by God, for a unique purpose. This purpose gets hindered because of the curse of sin that you inherited from Adam. The curse affects <u>every</u> part of you. It causes an infirmity of spirit, soul, and body- an infirmity with only *one* Healer: the Lord God of heaven. He says, "I am the Lord Who heals you!" (Exodus 15:26 AMP)

Spirit Healing

Your eternal spirit is healed the moment you accept Jesus and receive His gift of eternal life. The moment you defeat eternal death through Christ's blood, your spirit comes into its healing. It is a one-time event. When you make Christ the King of your heart, recognizing your need for Him to cleanse you from sin, you inherit His righteousness. What an inheritance! Your sins are wiped off your record so you may approach the Father without stain, without blemish. You are made alive forever. When a person is made new in Christ, the old creation is gone. The old spiritual condition has passed away; he is fresh and new. *A new creation!* (II Corinthians 5:17)

Body Healing

If your spirit has been healed through salvation in Jesus, your body will also be healed--ALL the way. It will happen when the Lord Jesus returns to resurrect His followers and bring them into total newness. Heaven and Earth will be renewed, and the saints in Christ will also be renewed. In *BODY!* I Corinthians 15 is very clear about this: "The dead in Christ will be raised imperishable, immune from decay, and shall be transformed. This perishable part must put on the imperishable nature; this mortal part that is capable of dying must put on immortality."[1]

Revelation 21 is clear about it too: "There will be no more death or mourning or crying or pain. The old order of things (will have) passed away."[2]

Whatever your ailment, whatever your infirmity of body is in this life, the Lord WILL heal you! If not in this life, in the life to come. *What a glorious hope!* He promises His people, "(My words) are life to those who find them, and health to one's whole body."[3] In Exodus 23:25 God promises, "I will bless you and take sickness away from you." All physical healing is dictated by Him. Healing from our cuts, our bruises, from colds and infections. God allows us to be healed of these things even now. But it is just a glimpse of what is yet to come.

SOUL HEALING

For the rest of this chapter and all of the next, I will describe some things God has shown me about soul healing. The thing about soul healing that is different from body and spirit healing is that it does not happen in an instant. *It is a continuing process.* A process that we are in right now. The process continues until our time of death. You can witness mighty, miraculous acts of healing in your mind, your will, your emotions- like what I have described in some of the previous chapters. Soul healing is what we <u>all</u> need DAILY. Even HOURLY. We can enter into it NOW. We don't have to wait for heaven! *Soul healing is heaven coming down to us, right here, right now.* Jesus didn't just die to heal your spirit and give you a renewed physical body free of sickness and pain. Jesus doesn't want you to be sick in your soul! He resurrected so that you will have a *renewed SOUL*--RIGHT <u>NOW</u>! Thank You, Jesus!

My most memorable instruction about soul healing came from a series of teachings and a divine encounter... one warm weekend in June 2011....

The idea of two days and nights alone with Mark was so inviting; I was giddy with excitement. It had been four years since we'd had a getaway like this. We would leave Friday as soon as I got off work. We would drop the kids off at friends' homes and we'd be off to White Salmon, Washington where we would gather with other Christ followers for a special weekend seminar. The focus of the seminar was *healing*. We would be there Friday evening and all day and evening on Saturday. A special speaker would be there, named Katie Souza. A former drug user and dealer, Katie had done some time in prison, where she met Jesus. She grew close to Him and began teaching His Word to her fellow female inmates. Now she has a recovery ministry in Arizona, called Expected End Ministries.[4] She helps ex-felons and recovering drug addicts find their way to new life and new hope in Jesus Christ.

I knew very little about Katie Souza, and I was very skeptical about going such a long way to hear her speak. But Mark had shared with me some of her writings and teachings on healing. I was interested and wanted to keep an open mind. "I'll go to this meeting, " I thought, "but if she starts blowing 'the breath of God' on people to make them fall down, I might have to bail." I was pleased just to be going to the meeting with Mark-- to be going *anywhere* with Mark. This whole thing was his idea. I didn't know how he would last through it. But I'd leave that part to God.

Mark was very excited to be there that night. I think he wanted to be healed there. I think he was hoping for a miracle. And deep down, maybe I was too. *"Lord, show me if this is truth or a facade. Let me know if this is not truly from You. I don't want to be led away from Your truth, God."*

The whole way to White Salmon we talked and listened to music, marveling at the picturesque scenes along the Columbia River Gorge. Just like so many good old times back in Alaska. It was a beautiful day in early June. The sun was shining, its light glistening through trees and on the waterways we passed over on the 90-minute drive.

About half-way through the trip, I realized I had forgotten to bring along my pain medicine. I had left it at work trying to get out of there in a hurry. This was a bad thing (I thought) because I had been having terrible pain in my right foot for about a month- and had been managing it regularly with Tylenol with codeine. I'd already sustained other injuries to my feet, which had healed over the past two years with therapy and multiple cortisone shots. But this pain was a recent, new pain that had come out of nowhere during a time of compounding stress over the past couple of weeks. The pain was on the top of my foot, the instep- shooting out from my toes up to my ankle- causing my whole leg to feel sore.

"My codeine, Mark! I forgot it!"

We looked at each other without speaking, giving each other that surprised "Oh, no!" expression, but knowing we absolutely could *not* go back. It was too far and we would miss the meeting.

"Oh, well- I'll just have to bear it," I thought. "I hope I can stand up for the whole worship time."

My foot pain had become so extreme the past three weeks that at times it affected my walking and caused me discomfort while wearing certain shoes and while standing. I'd been teaching all week and had only one week of school left before summer break. I was tired. Normally on a night like tonight, I'd be putting my foot up, icing it and resting it. But not tonight. That would just have to wait.

We found a seat in the crowded sanctuary. Music played and there was an air of expectancy in the room. Many people were smiling, praying, talking together, and reading the Bible in preparation for the night's event. Mark and I chatted with a few people we knew who had also made the trip to hear the special teaching. The seats were filling up fast. When it was time to start, Katie Souza was introduced and expressed her gratitude for her invitation there, and for our attendance.

"We're going to start this night off with an extended time of praise and worship," Katie said.

"Oh, great," I thought. "My poor foot." It was already having spasms and throbbing. *Ugh.*

"While we are worshipping the Lord tonight, I am going to be praying for each person in this room," Katie announced. "I am going to pray that spirits, souls, and bodies be healed in Jesus' name tonight."

And so, we began to worship God as Katie began to pray for us. The songs were lively and I loved how everyone around me seemed to be singing from their hearts, the way I like to do. The summer breeze blew through the sanctuary, through open windows on both sides of the building, and I began to fall into a wonderful time of blocking everything out except God. At first I was distracted by my pain- and by the sight of Katie at the front praying. She wasn't singing along. She was stretching her hand out over the congregation, and looking at each row of people as her lips were moving, but no one could hear her over the music. "That's different," I thought. I hadn't seen a speaker do *that* before.

After standing to sing several songs, I was no longer distracted by anything. All that was on my mind was the Lord. I had come to that place where I was just getting completely lost in Him. That was the place where it happened.

I raised my arm while singing, and a warmth came over me. It felt the exact same as the warmth I often felt when I took my narcotic pain reliever. The warmth started at my head and went down through my body until I felt it in my feet. It lingered for several moments. I felt really good. So alive and so relaxed. Then I noticed that my foot stopped hurting. Just suddenly. It just *stopped hurting*. Still singing, I moved it around a bit. No pain. I flexed and lifted my toes. No pain. A feeling of relief came over me. This was the first time that foot hadn't hurt *at all*, in *weeks*.

Hmm...interesting... I thought to myself as we continued praising the Lord awhile longer. Then we sat down to listen to the teaching.

That night I learned so much (which I will share with you now). I learned about our soul wounds...and the power of Jesus to heal them...

SOUL WOUNDS AND THE DUNAMIS

God's Word speaks about "excellence of soul" (I Corinthians 4:19-20) and a prosperous, healthy soul (III John 1:2). By contrast, a tormented, traumatized Job speaks about his *bitterness* of soul (Job 7:11, 10:1). Barren, childless Hannah, when pleading with God to let her give birth to a son, wept sorely through her prayer, in bitterness of soul (I Samuel 1:10). David, after sinning against God sexually with Bathsheba, lamented in agony; his soul cried out in pain (Psalm 38). These parts of the Bible indicate that our souls can be sick, and they can be made well.

There's really no denying this; I am sure you can relate to this as I can. Consider how sick you have felt at times of your life, sick in your *emotions*- and how healthy you have felt emotionally in other times. If you've ever felt anguish or despair because of a wrongdoing (committed by you or someone else), you know what soul sickness is. *Soul sickness is caused by soul wounds.*[5] Soul excellence (soul wellness), however, comes when those wounds are healed. But what heals them? It's not like we can apply a medical ointment to them. They are invisible. But there's no denying they're there.

"Excellence of soul", as spoken of in the Bible, is a *force*. It's an energy, a moral power. Studying the original Greek texts from New Testament passages that mention soul excellence (soul wellness), we find a specific word...the same word that names the power of Christ to rise from the dead...

...the word is **DUNAMIS**.

DUNAMIS is the same word from which we get our English words "dynamite" and "dynamo". It is POWER. STRENGTH. ABILITY. But not just any power; it is the power over all other powers! Dunamis is not an earthly power; it is <u>divine</u> power. It's GOD power! Dunamis is the power that will usher in the Kingdom of God (Mark 9:1). It is what Jesus told the Sadducees they were lacking (Matthew 22:29), the reason for their spiritual blindness. Jesus' dunamis is what will surround Him when He returns in the clouds to meet the saints in the air (Matthew 24:30). It is what makes the impossible possible and casts out evil spirits (John 15:5; Luke 4:36). Dunamis is the power that raised Jesus from the dead and performed healing miracles during His earthly ministry (Acts 10:38). It's the power that gives us excellence of soul. It _is_ excellence of soul.

We inherit this strong excellence of soul by His resurrection.[6]

And when applied to our soul wounds, dunamis is the force that heals them.

Inheriting the Dunamis

In order for a person to inherit something, someone else must die. A will is not in effect until the person who declared it expires. When Jesus died on the cross, His "will" for our spiritual healing was put into effect. When He resurrected from that death, His "will" for our _soul healing_ was put into effect. The Apostle Paul understood this. He describes it in I Corinthians 15:43, saying that we are sown in infirmity and weakness (powerlessness), but we are resurrected (in Christ) in strength and endued with power (DUNAMIS)! By receiving Christ's atoning sacrifice, our spirits are made well forever. By receiving the power of His resurrection, our souls are made well forever too. Starting _NOW!_

Some of us look at the cross again and again....we think about it, we sing about it, we read books about it...and we wonder why our souls are still sick. How can we be so focused on Christ's cross and still feel so hurt and rejected in our minds? How can we walk around with "poochy-lip disease", sulking and floundering in all our woes, when we've accepted His salvation? The answer is... we aren't looking enough at His _resurrection_. We must look at His _resurrection power_ too! We must look to it just as we look to the cross!

See, when Jesus died, He took on Himself the sin of the world. But He also took on the FULL BURDEN of every soul wound we would ever have. The horrible feelings we have because of abuse and neglect. He bore those! The heartache of betrayal, the grief of loss. _He suffered those wounds in His soul!_ He offered His soul as the Sacrifice, not only to cover the acts of sin we would commit, but every effect of those sins that would plague our minds and emotions. Jesus POURED OUT His soul. (Isaiah 53:10-12) This is worded this way so we would know that His suffering was not only physical. It was a mental, emotional anguish He endured on our behalf. When He conquered His own murder, all those soul wounds He had taken on were HEALED in that victory. In His resurrection, He was raised to newness- allowing a transfer to take place.[7] A transfer of HIS excellence of soul (His dunamis!) -- *to us!*

By Christ's death we are healed from our spirit wound (sin). This is the *first* part of our inheritance in Him. By His resurrection we are healed from our soul wounds (the effects of sin). This is the *second* part of our inheritance in Him!

We are literally *inheritors in light.* (Colossians 1:12) Partakers of His resurrection power, which is His light! "In Christ you have been brought to fullness. Your whole self ruled by the flesh- was put off when you were...buried with Him, (and) also *RAISED* with Him through your faith in the working of God- Who raised Him from the dead." (Colossians 2:9-12 NIV)

I believe the glory light of Christ is what shined out of Him when he healed the demon-possessed boy in Mark 9:15. His face was glistening; His "whole person" was glowing with light and people were astounded by it. I believe the glory light of Christ is what shined out of Stephen at the time of his stoning. It's what burned in the hearts of the disciples as they healed people and cast out demons in Jesus' name- and gave themselves in martyrdom to Him. I don't believe His glory light is gone from the earth! I don't think it went away! It's *still* here, accessible to us-- that we may overcome- and lead others to overcome- all the ravaging effects of sin in this world. Hallelujah!

SEEING THE GLORY LIGHT OF CHRIST

Looking to the blood of Christ is essential for the cleansing of our sin. But we must look at Christ not only in His suffering at Calvary, but also standing outside the tomb three days later...and standing in front of Thomas as he touched His wounds...and ascending into the clouds...and coming back the same way...and seated at His throne... IN THE LIGHT OF HIS GLORY!

The light of Christ's glory has the power to renew our hearts, to bring our sick souls back to wholeness! Hourly, daily, weekly, monthly, yearly. We need His LIGHT, the POWER of His resurrection, to heal up the hurts we sustain by the sinful acts we do and the sinful acts others do that hurt us. The dunamis power of Christ is the reason He exudes LIGHT. It's not just that He *possesses* light. He _IS_ light! His light is the power that defeats darkness! And it has been given to _us_! WOW! We have access to it when we have cleansed ourselves of our idols (as I will describe in the next chapter). A clean temple (heart and body) can position us to effectively bask in His light-- literally IMMERSE ourselves in it- to hear from Him and experience His radiance. He is ready to reveal His brightness to us in spectacular ways!

Jesus is the Light of the world, "the true and genuine, steadfast and perfect Light that came into the world to illumine every person." (John 1:9) But He is also the Light of heaven. The Bright Morning Star. (Revelation 22:16) Is it any wonder that God used an intensely bright star to direct men to Jesus at the time of His birth?! How appropriate! No lamps are needed in heaven because *Jesus* is there. (Revelation 21:23) He is the LIGHT OF LIFE that eradicates darkness. (John 8:12) When darkness is eradicated in us, healing can take place. When the Lord's enemies are destroyed, when the strongholds fall, the light of the sun will be seven times brighter, like the light of seven days concentrated into one. And the Lord will bind up the hurt of His people, and heal their sin wounds. (Isaiah 30:25-26) Jesus is the Sun of Righteousness (not just the "SON"; but the "SUN!") Who arises with _healing_ in His beams, healing which He gives to those who revere and worshipfully fear His name. (Malachi 4:2)

That Friday night in White Salmon was the first time I understood the connection between the LIGHT of Christ and my need for healing. The LIGHT of Christ is His power, His glory. You and I can place ourselves in it, whenever we want. I encourage you to do this; I have done it often and it is very empowering!

Set aside a space and time to think <u>only</u> on the light of the glory of Christ Jesus.[8] Read about His glory in the Bible. Sing about it. *Ask Him to show it to you.* I believe you will see it manifested in your life, just as I have in mine. When we focus in to see the beaming light that shines from Jesus' hands, His face, "His whole person"- we are turning our minds away from all earthly things that distract us from His perfect beauty. Getting our minds focused on Him alone brings us to a place where we can be loosed from the effects of our own sin and sin that others have committed against us. THAT is healing, and it can be done again and again until we are at Christ's side. How wonderfully familiar it will be to look upon His light in heaven, if we have gazed upon it many times here in the now!

God's light grants us spiritual discernment. Divine power helps us to see things we could not otherwise see. It can help us see past our own sinful acts into the roots where they were born. It can even help us see sin roots in others so we may encourage them better, ministering to them and praying more effectively for their healing.

The glory light of Christ has healed me in my soul. And in my thankfulness I proclaim, "*You* cause my lamp to be lighted and to shine! The Lord my God illumines my darkness!" (Psalm 18:28 AMP) I pray this will be *your* proclamation too. I hope that you grab hold of the resurrection power of Jesus, see the glowing light of His glory, and receive healing in all parts of you, in His name!

CHAPTER 18

BLEEDING HANDS THAT HEAL ME

"By *His* wounds we are healed." Isaiah 53:5 (NIV)

That warm June night in White Salmon, I didn't say anything to anyone about my foot pain suddenly going away. I didn't even tell Mark. I wanted to see how long this "healing" would really last. I had doubt in my heart, even after everything God had already shown me in my life. *Is this really You, God, or am I being deceived somehow by my enemy?* I wouldn't have to wait long for Him to answer me.

Pain rode home with us that night, but sat handcuffed in the back seat. Mark and I were not about to let Pain steal the joy of this exciting revelation we'd just received. The whole way home, Mark and I discussed everything we learned, how God spoke to both of us so clearly, how He showed us new things about His power. We were impressed and astonished by the reach of His glowing hands in those hours.

I wanted to tell Mark about my foot. But my doubt was hindering me from testifying about it just yet. "Let's just see how it feels in the morning," I thought. The mornings were always the worst. The foot was always terribly stiff and extra sore the first hour of the day. I usually had to limp down the hallway from the bedroom to the kitchen to get my morning coffee, as the tendons "stretched out" after the stillness of my night sleep. It was the same morning after morning. Why would tomorrow morning be any different? I had my doubts the pain relief would last beyond that night. "Maybe I was just exhilarated from the great worship time," I thought to myself, as I went to sleep that night.

The next morning, to my pleasant surprise, I awoke to a pain-free foot. I got out of bed and walked to the bathroom. No pain. Got my coffee. No pain. Showered. No pain. I didn't even need to take ibuprofen before we left to return to White Salmon. "_Now this is getting real!_" I thought.

We got on the road early, fresh and ready for more revelation. I figured it was time to tell Mark.

"Hey, um...guess what?! I'm pretty sure God healed my foot last night."

"For real!?"

"Yes, for real. It hasn't hurt at all since the worship time last night." And I told Mark what had happened. I told him about the warmth and the sudden dissipation of discomfort which had lasted through the night and into this morning. The pain was really gone. This was not my imagination. It was my miracle.

During the first Saturday meeting, Katie Souza asked if anyone had been healed physically in some way the night before. "Come on up to the front, all you who were healed by God last night!" she said. Several people stood and began making their way to the front. I just sat there, wondering, "Was I _really_ healed? Is this for real?"

Both Mark and my friend John were sitting next to me, coaxing me to get my healed self up there to the front of the sanctuary. "Go on, Davida! You were healed, weren't you? You gotta _testify_! God will bless you and others through your testimony!" I hesitated quite a bit, still affected by doubt. But after a few more moments, I decided, "OK, alright! I'll go up there."

I proceeded to tell Katie- and all the other people in the church that morning- about my foot healing the night before. About how I had forgotten my pain medicine, so I would be able to feel the pain intensely and then to feel the sharp contrast of *no* pain, so I knew when the pain had left me. (I knew by this time that forgetting my pain pills was not an "accident".) I noted aloud to everyone there that I hadn't needed *any* pain medicine since the worship time the night before, and that I did believe God had worked a miracle of healing in my physical body.

Then Katie placed her hand on my head and prayed for me- in genuineness and in the power of God's Spirit. She spoke hope and divine assurance into my life. She thanked God for healing my foot and for what He would show me through that encounter. And as she prayed, I heard the Lord telling me, "*I* did this. This is real. This is *Me*! *I* healed you. Come into My *full* healing, Davida. There is more to come."

In those moments, I completely stopped doubting this came from Him. I embraced Him again as I had done many times before, but this time He was revealing His goodness to me in a new way- as my Healer. All the things that had been stressing me out in the past few weeks were melting *off*. I was letting God seize hold of me with glory, with His healing hands. I felt incredibly safe, incredibly loved.

"Now that I have your attention, Davida, I want to show you something *else...*"

I sat down again and a few minutes later, the teaching resumed. That day I would learn that something more was required of me, for my soul's full healing. It would go beyond accessing Christ's dunamis. Beyond basking in His glorious light. *It would involve a cleansing.*

Action Required

A few times in Scripture, when a person was healed physically, some *action* was required on their part. They were asked to <u>do</u> something, to demonstrate a measure of faith and obedience, before their healing would take effect.

Naaman was one of those people. A "mighty man of valor", Naaman was a very successful man- who also was a leper (II Kings 5). When Naaman heard that God's prophet Elisha could possibly bring God's healing upon him, he went to Elisha- expecting him to wave his hand over him to be miraculously and instantaneously healed (verse 11). But instead, Elisha told him to go wash himself in the Jordan River SEVEN times, and *then* he would be healed. This made Naaman very angry. Why should *he* have to do anything to get healed? Couldn't he just stand there and get his miracle? Why the crazy request that he go do something that didn't seem to make much sense? And why the Jordan River? That river was not as clean as other rivers in the area! Why would he have to dip in that nasty river in order to be made clean? That didn't make sense! Naaman stomped off in a rage, throwing a tantrum at first. But then, in his desperation, he went to the river and followed Elisha's orders. Naaman washed himself seven times in that muddy river. And God healed his leprosy. His skin was so well restored that it was like the skin of a little child (verse 14). Naaman proclaimed that the God of Israel had to be the one true God. God had unveiled Himself to Naaman in a special way. But the healing wasn't a total "freebie".

Naaman had to do something he didn't want to do.

He had to be cleansed, God's way.

Centuries later, a man who was born blind had an encounter with Jesus. Jesus would demonstrate His glory by healing his blindness -- to show God's hand at work in the world. Before performing the miracle, Jesus said to His disciples, "I am the world's Light."[1] (Remember, light is required for vision.) Then He spat on the ground and made mud with the dirt and His saliva. He spread the spit-mud mixture as an ointment, directly on the man's eyes. He then asked him to go wash in the pool of Siloam. When the man washed off the mud, he opened his eyes and could see. For the first time in his life. Then the healed man testified to others, about how Jesus had healed him. (John 9: 1-11)

In both of these instances, men were asked to perform an

action before they would be healed. The action they were asked to perform involved CLEANSING. *God's way.* It involved WASHING OFF THE DIRT. Getting rid of the slimy mud that covered their infirmities. *Why did God do this?* Why didn't He just heal them by waving His hand over their heads? I have contemplated this a lot, and the Lord has shown me three reasons why He did it this way:

1. The healing would come in the way determined by the <u>Healer</u>, *not* by the one being healed.
2. The healing would result *after* <u>obedience</u> was demonstrated by the one being healed.
3. Washing off the mud represented another cleansing that ALL men need.

SOUL CLEANSING.

True healing of our wounded souls is accomplished when our souls are first cleansed. Soul cleansing takes place when we see our "dirt" and purposely wash it off. But not with water. With the blood of Jesus. How can we wash off "dirt" that we can't even see? Well, we have to get in a place where we can "see" it in our soul and spirit. The place where God will show you your dirt is in focused, intense prayer. Then, once we see it and get rid of it by Jesus' blood, we can position ourselves to really see His glory light shine into our being and into our relationships. To receive the healing He wants to bring us.

The *cleansing* is the required action.

But, what "dirt" are we cleansing ourselves of?

Idols.

Yep, you heard me. IDOLS.

THE TEMPLE IDOLS

You might be saying, as I said when I first began studying about idolatry, "*I* don't *have* any idols!" You might be thinking idols are those little metal or wood statues that people pray to in some religions. "I don't have any little metal statues. I don't pray to anyone but God. Therefore I am idol-free." I used to say that. I knew for a long time that idols were not just little statues. I knew what idols really were. And I *still* thought I was idol-free! But God showed me otherwise. He showed me my pride, my foolishness in thinking that nothing in my life could be separating me from the fullness of God's glory in my life. I believe that EVERYONE has *some* kind of idol they give place to. Let me explain...

When you focus on something enough mentally or emotionally, it burns an image onto your soul. Just as your eye or a camera will record an image of an object, so our souls "take a picture" of something that is taking the place of God in our minds. We keep looking at it, over and over. This image- this idol- is *anything* or *anyone* we give precedence to mentally and emotionally (over God). It's that thing (or person) you just "can't stop thinking about". It's that thing (or person) you think about or desire more than God.[2] Eventually, it can replace God altogether as the love and ruler of your heart.

It could be money. Whether you're rich or poor or somewhere in the middle, money can very easily become an idol. It could be sex. Or a person you're sexually or emotionally infatuated with. It can be a relationship- even a God-given relationship like a spousal relationship or a relationship with your own child. Your idol might be some material thing. Or your job. Even a personal ministry. It can be good things, like your kids or your health. It can be food. Alcohol. Or some other drug. It can be some gifting God gave you. Your music, your art, your writing. *It's whatever thing(s) that you choose to give first place to again and again in your mind, will, and emotions - in a way that "satisfies" you where God is supposed to be the One satisfying you.*

We tend to cling to our idols thinking they will satisfy and fulfill our souls, thinking they will heal our soul wounds. But they just end up making new soul wounds in us, or making the ones that were already there even deeper. Our idols sustain our soul wounds. Just like dirt in a flesh wound. They prevent our healing.[3]

I believe that idolatry- in *any* form- is used by Satan's demons (evil, unclean spirits) to bring about our physical, mental, and spiritual demise. The same demons of idolatry that afflicted the evil kings in the Old Testament are still at work in our world today. Demons of pride, lust, and greed. Demons of perversion, adultery, murder. They are at work in leaders of nations, leaders of churches, leaders of homes and families. They are at work in *every single person* alive on this earth. As we set our eyes on images of "false gods", giving our souls over to forces not associated with God's Spirit, we are setting ourselves up for vulnerability to demonic influence.

But there is hope for us! All our idols can be covered by the blood of Jesus, by a purposeful, willful covering- then cast out of our minds and bodies (God's temple) by His power and replaced with His glory!

Desecration of God's temple is noted several times in the Bible. A temple of God was defiled when something evil (contrary to the Word of the Lord) was brought in and permitted to have a place there. If images of other gods were brought into the temple of Yahweh, they were an abomination to Him! *They did not belong in the place of His holiness.* A desecrated temple had to be *cleansed.* It had to be cleaned up and re-arranged back the way that God had ordained it to be from the beginning. King Hezekiah knew this. He lived in a time when the leaders of Judah had given themselves to pagan gods and idolatry. One of the first things he did after becoming king was to restore God's temple to its original purpose, according to God's design instructions. Hezekiah and the Levite priests removed all the "rubbish" from the temple that had been brought in by the previous leaders- including his father Ahaz, one of the most notoriously corrupted kings in Israel's history. The temple was such a mess- in need of so much consecration- that the task took Hezekiah's crew over two weeks to complete. Once the idols were removed, Hezekiah oversaw a large-scale sacrifice of 28 animals- rams, goats, lambs, and bulls. The priests took the blood from these sacrifices and sprinkled it all over the altar in the temple, multiple times. Wherever worship of false gods had taken place, blood was spilt to cover that idolatry, "to atone for all of Israel". (II Chronicles 29)

The reason this story is critically important to us today is the powerful analogy it holds for us. We are now the *living temple* of God's Holy Spirit! Our hearts are where He dwells, where He is worshipped, where sacrifices are made unto Him. But our temples have been desecrated by the sins of our idolatry! "For though you wash yourself with lye and use much soap, your iniquity and guilt are still upon you. You are spotted, dirty, and stained before Me, says the Lord." (Jeremiah 2:22 AMP)

When we put other things before God, we defile His temple. We do things with His temple that should never be done! What an abomination! How can we expect God to heal our innermost being- or our physical body- as we bring idols- demonic forces- into His temple?

Cleansing your temple means first repenting <u>of your own idolatry</u>.

> *Repenting of your idolatry is recognizing anything you have made an idol in your heart- and <u>removing</u> it from your heart, God's temple. Ask God to reveal to you exactly what your idol is, if you don't already know. You may have more than one; maybe many. Once you've identified your idol (or idols) by God's Spirit, visualize its removal from your heart! This means you are putting the idol off <u>without intent to pick it up again</u>. It means agreeing with God that this idol is keeping you from closeness with Him.*

Then, visualize the blood of Jesus Christ covering the place your idol had been.

> *This may sound weird, but I believe it is powerful imagery in our souls. Focus on the blood of Jesus,*

to take the place of that idol that had been in your
soul. Visualize Christ's blood cleansing your heart
of that specific sin- and <u>*atoning*</u> *for it.*

We may pray to ask God to help us "stop thinking about" things we know are taking precedence over Christ, in our minds. But if that prayer is half-hearted, without our genuine intention to eradicate the problem, *our souls will remain in infirmity.* The cleansing action must be one that *we* willingly perform. Just like Naaman and the blind man washing themselves, *we* must purge our idols from the temple! *We're* the ones who have to do the repenting! *We* must look away from our idols and look only at the blood of Christ to cover them! Then, in our cleanliness, we can look upon the light of His glory to heal us from the wounds those idols have made in our being. The cleansing may come instantaneously, or gradually-- but spiritual freedom <u>*will*</u> come as we do this sincerely before a holy, righteous God!

THE BLOOD AND THE LIGHT *APPLIED*

That second night in White Salmon, in the last meeting of the conference, we had a time of prayerful focus on these things we had learned and thought about all day. My eyes were closed as I talked to God, repeatedly asking Him to reveal my soul's idols. After several minutes, with eyes still closed, I had a vision of my kitchen pantry being opened. My hands were in front of me, and I could see the many boxes of diet food. It was my pantry exactly how it looked at that time. I had been on a special program to help me lose weight. One of those commercial programs. A great program, to be sure. But I had been looking at it to heal me, to make me well physically. I had looked to those diet food boxes to heal me- instead of God. *Had that diet program become an idol in my heart?* Then I saw my own hand sprinkling blood on those diet food boxes. Until they were covered in it. The blood dripped over the boxes, covering them completely. Then the vision ended.

God spoke to me in those moments, telling me that HE was able to heal my lifelong struggle with weight gain. He told me that my obesity battle wasn't just physical; it was *spiritual*. It related to my soul wounds, even ones that originated in my early childhood-when I felt picked on and ugly and horribly different from everyone else. "Stop looking to everything but Me, to heal you of this infirmity," He was saying. "Let Me satisfy you completely. Let Me be your everything. Don't let food be your comfort. *I* am your Comforter! Stop looking to diet products to help you be well. Let *Me* heal you!"

As I stepped into the light of Jesus' resurrection then, I knew that God could renew my physical body just as He was renewing my soul. He could raise me to newness of bodily health. The foot healing was His way of getting my attention, getting things started. *That pain has never returned to me.*

The next few months, I made changes to my diet. Small changes at first, then big ones. I began eating less processed food. More whole foods, more raw foods--fruits and vegetables, beans, and nuts. *God's* foods, *not* man's. I began to feel better than I'd felt in years. I lost weight. My physical stamina was increased and I exercised regularly (easier now, with my foot pain gone). My physical body was prospering just as my soul was prospering! It was amazing. During that time, several people at various different times told me that I looked healthier than they'd ever seen me. A few of them told me I looked like I was *glowing.* It was JESUS! *He* was shining brightly in me! I had been freed of the bondage of diet drinks and powders, special soups, and bottles of bitter pills. I was in prayer and God's Word every day. I was eating God's food both spiritually and physically. I was thriving from the inside out!

At the end of that summer, on the very last day of my medical insurance (not coincidentally), I got up in the morning and walked to the living room to make a phone call. After the phone call, I stood up from my sitting position on the couch, and my back suddenly began to spasm. I felt shooting pain in my lower back and leg; then what felt like multiple Charley horses in my calf and behind my knee. My lower leg grew numb, and the pain was amplified considerably throughout the course of that morning. It was my first experience with sciatica and vertebral disc herniation. On the very day that I was losing my medical insurance. No pain medicine, no imaging, no doctor visits would be easily obtainable now. At first I felt fear. *What if this doesn't go away? What if this leads into some bigger problem? What if something's really wrong with my back? What I become disabled like Mark? How will we live? How will we get by?*

The Lord quickly rebuked me in my spirit for thinking that way. Everything I had learned just three months earlier, about healing, now needed to be put into practice. I needed to be healed physically, but I was also allowing doubt to creep into my heart again. I needed to trust and look to HIM ALONE to bring healing to me.

For about three days, I could not move much without excruciating pain. I lied in bed and prayed for much of that time. I didn't need to understand fully why that was happening to me. I needed to be faithful in removing the idols in my heart, His temple. I needed to look at the cross of Jesus and apply His blood to wash me, to cleanse me from the influences of my sin. I needed to look at the resurrection of Jesus, to stare intently at His glory light, to see Him in the brilliance of His dunamis. So I did that. Within a week, the sciatica subsided. The pain went away. For the next two years, I had no medical insurance. (This was not by choice; it was how things were working out with my jobs at the time.) I received no medical care for the problem in my spine. What I did receive was *God's caring for me in His own way.* It was enough! *HE* was enough!

What I have presented here is not some magic trick for you to perform and- "poof!"- be healed of every affliction instantly in your life. Nor am I urging you to go drop your current medical insurance plan! I have tried to describe some ways God has made His Word very real to me. *Revelation of the sweetest kind.*

The Lord may choose to withhold healing (in this life) of a physical problem you have. Trust that He is using it for a higher purpose, beyond what you can see right now. But I don't believe He withholds soul and spirit healing (in this life) from anyone who is consistently seeking it in accordance with God's Word. It is ready for you. Receive it!

I believe the Lord has healed my spirit fully (at the time of my salvation) and now He is progressively healing me of soul and body infirmities, as I learn how to *see* more and more of Him in my life. I believe that my soul-and-spirit health directly affects my body health. I believe that God cares about me. *And He cares about you!*

You might be thinking, "Sure, I'd like to get rid of _____ (insert the name of your idol). But it's just been with me too long. I don't think I can just cast it off and be done with it. It's too much a part of me now." **No idol is too powerful or too big in our souls for Christ's blood to wash away!** Apply His power of resurrection (His dunamis) to *keep it away!* BELIEVE THAT GOD can do a major work in you, right NOW! You might need to cast that idol off multiple times in a row, in a day or even in a moment. This might be a daily thing you do. *Do it!* Replace that idol with the light of the Lord! Soon His light will take over in you, and that old thing you struggled *not* to give place to- will be a thing of your past. That's victory. That's *healing*!

If you need soul healing right now in your life, call on Jesus! Consider how much He cares for you and wants your soul to prosper in radiant excellence. Cry out to Him in your affliction. Let His blood cover your sin! Let His resurrection power touch you and illuminate you, that you may be made whole by His hand, healed in your body, spirit, and soul-- in Jesus' name!

"I will cut off the names of the idols, and
they shall no more be remembered.
And I will remove the unclean spirit."
-the Word of the Lord spoken in Zechariah 13:2 (AMP)

CHAPTER 19

ARMS OF PROTECTION

"The eternal God is your refuge and dwelling place, and underneath (you) are the everlasting arms." He is holding your hand. Deuteronomy 33:27 (AMP); Isaiah 41:13

The earliest nightmare I remember having was the spider tree dream. My family lived in a country log cabin at the time. Small bugs and spiders often wandered into my room from the outside, through tiny cracks or holes in the wood walls. I can't remember which came first: my recurring bad dream or my fear of spiders. They seemed to come at the same time. I was only 5, but I remember that nightmare vividly. I was climbing up a tree, a perfect tree-climbing kind of tree, on a nice clear day. There wasn't anything in the dream but the tree and the blue sky above, the ground below, and me. When I got about half-way up the tree, the trunk suddenly turned into a solid column of large brown spiders. I had to hang onto the tree or I would fall. I couldn't let go, and I couldn't get down before the spiders would be crawling all over me, in my hair, on my arms. I'd try to start climbing down, but I couldn't move. I was paralyzed with fear and could do nothing but freeze there and let the spiders cover me. Then I'd wake up and be so creeped out, I could hardly breathe. I'd look around my dark room, at the holes in the wood walls. *Would those spiders come through the walls and cover me in my bed just like they covered me in the tree? Would they bite me? Hurt me?*

One night when I awoke from that dream, I sat up in my bed and prayed to Jesus to make me not feel scared anymore. I asked Him to take away the fear I felt. And He <u>did</u>! He ministered to me as He did to Isaiah, to whom He promised, *"Fear not; there is nothing to fear! For I am with you. Do not look around you in terror and be dismayed. For I am your God! I will strengthen and help you. I will hold you up and retain you with My victorious right hand of rightness and justice."* (Isaiah 41:10 AMP)

I went back to sleep, and I never dreamed about the spider tree again.

This may seem like a silly little story, but I believe Jesus was revealing- even then- His power to deliver me from fear. Now I know that fear can be used by demons to torment people in their souls. A well-known acronym for F.E.A.R. is <u>F</u>alse <u>E</u>vidence <u>A</u>ppearing <u>R</u>eal. How true that is! Fear is so often based on appearances, imaginations.

God delivered me from several fears even at a tender young age. Throughout my childhood, I always knew Jesus was watching over me and keeping me safe. Any time I thought of something scary, I'd pray, "Jesus, please make me not scared of that anymore!" And sometimes I would visualize Him right there next to me; I would try to see *Him* in my mind instead of whatever was scaring me. Praying that way and "seeing Him" near me, protecting me from the scary thing, always calmed my fear. It worked <u>every</u> time. I *still* do that. And it *still* works!

Our family would sometimes visit the home of an elderly couple we knew. They lived in my grandparents' neighborhood in

Pennsauken, New Jersey. Their house had the coolest old antique wooden horse that used to be part of a carousel. It was colorful, shiny, huge, and so beautiful. They would let me sit in the saddle and pretend I was riding a real horse. But the horse wasn't what I loved most about visiting that house. It was the big painting of Jesus that hung by their front door (a famous image created by Warner Sallman[1]). That picture was the first thing I'd see when entering their house, and the last thing I'd see when leaving. I always felt safe there, like Jesus was in that house, and it was because of that picture. It was a very real comfort, the presence of Christ being invited into that home. His presence made me feel safe.

When I got much older and more conscious of how the world works, I developed a fear of stalkers. You know, the creepy men who stalk women to rape or kill them- or both. When I started driving, I never liked to be alone at night in the car. *What if I broke down and a stalker came and hurt me? What if I was walking to my car and he chased me and I couldn't run fast enough to get away?* Though these fears were real, they were based on imaginations which manifested into dark illusions of frightening things that *could* happen. I would play out the scenes of the crimes in my mind. These imaginations would have paralyzed me spiritually- if not for Jesus. After a time, I began praying to Jesus EVERY TIME a stalker-man thought entered my mind. I would ask Jesus to strike down that imagination *as soon* as it entered my thoughts. After praying like that several times in a row over a short period of time, the fear was gone. He took that paranoia away. Freed me of it completely. It has never returned.

Psalm 91 speaks of the safe refuge we have in the Lord. The way He delivers us from fear and shields us from harm. It describes how we can hide right under His wings and be safe. How He frees us from the terror of the night and the pestilence that stalks us in darkness. It speaks of God's angels guiding us out of harm's way, bearing us up on their hands so we won't get hurt. *A shield is held in the hand or fastened to the arm.* The Lord as our Shield gives us another picture of His strong arm, this time protecting us from danger.

The Lord has revealed Himself many times in my life by physically protecting me and my children with His steady hand...

The summer of 1995, I drove with two college friends from South Carolina to Jackson Hole, Wyoming. We would do the trip as a long haul in my Chrysler Dodge Caravan, stopping only for gas and food. The three of us would take turns driving. It was the middle of May. We were all very young and inexperienced drivers. Somewhere between the Laramie Mountains and the Grand Tetons, we found ourselves in a real pickle. The weather had changed from moderate to severe in just a few hours, as we made our way along the winding mountain pass roads. Snow began falling fast and fiercely, with high winds howling loudly outside our cozy little vehicle. We kept going, thinking we would just "drive through it". The steepness of the grades was extreme in some parts of the highway we were on. The road was slick with ice, and visibility was diminishing by the minute. There were few vehicles on the road. It was late at night and very dark. We had been driving a long time, but the danger of the situation made the three of us very awake. And very frightened. We were completely unprepared for an emergency. We had no cell phone, no road flares, no tire chains, no warm blankets or coats or boots. We crept along slowly until we could not see the lane separation anymore. We could hardly see the road. Everything was covered up with snow, snow that kept piling up as the wind blew it around in a dizzying swirl that felt like a tornado of blinding white.

"If we keep going, we're probably going to wreck the van!" I said, as the three of us agreed we ought to probably stop the vehicle and make a plan, possibly take our chances with waiting it out. We pulled over as much as we could, in what was left of the shoulder. *This snow is going to bury us for sure. What if we get stuck here? What if this blizzard lasts all night, and we freeze here in this little piece of dark highway?* I prayed that the Lord would help us not panic and get us to safety soon.

We had not sat there very long before a large freight truck came upon us. Moving as slowly as we had been, the truck was inching up the road to the place where we were. It passed us. But then, stopped. And backed up to the place where we were. A man- probably in his 50's- got out of the truck, obviously dressed for the weather much better than we were. He approached my driver's side window, and I rolled it down just enough to hear him speak. *What if this guy wants to rob us? Or hurt us? Steal my van and leave us out here in the snow?*

"Hey, you guys OK?" he asked, wincing from the wind and snowflakes hitting his face at all angles.

Not wanting to give him too much information (in case he was a stalker man, of course- because I hadn't been freed of that fear yet), I said, "Yes, we are fine. We haven't been stopped too long."

He then asked me a few questions which all seemed to have one thing in common: concern for our safety. This made me realize he probably was not going to hurt us. *Maybe this guy can help us get out of this.*

He asked me how much I had driven in snow. "Never," I said. It was true. I had *never* driven in those conditions in my life. I'd never really had training for it, either.

"You'd better just try to get to the next town," he said. "This storm is going to go on all night. You can't stay here like this!"

"Ya, but I can't see the road. I can't tell the road apart from the roadside."

"Don't worry about it," he assured me. "If you stay directly behind me, and let me lead the way, I can get you to the next little town where you can stay the night." He gave me instructions for how to handle the steep downhill grades. He made me explain it back to him, so he was sure I got it. "We're gonna go slow but steady," he said. "I'll get you out of this. Just don't lose me. Stay really close behind me. As close as you can safely."

"Thank you so much, sir!" I exclaimed, feeling very relieved already. We probably drove 15 or 20 miles like that, staying right on his tail as the lights of his truck illuminated the road in front of us. His truck was very large and had obviously plowed through this type of storm before. My little mini-van was tucked nicely in the pocket of air behind the back of his truck. I could not see the road, but I could see the truck. I just kept following it- until it led me to that green exit sign, and the lights of signs and buildings up ahead. The driver honked his horn and kept going, disappearing quickly from our sight. As we found the small hotel room that would provide us shelter and warm cozy beds for the night, we remarked on how miraculous the whole experience seemed. *Was that guy an angel? Could it be that truck was a chariot right out of heaven, sent to guide us to safety?* Maybe! But even if not, I do believe God directed that man and his truck at that exact time, to rescue us. To answer our prayers. I was extremely aware of God's protective hand holding us up that night. I thanked Him for watching over us like that. *"You're so good to us, Lord!"*

Another time, years later, I fell asleep at the wheel while driving home from work. My two children sat in the back seat. I hit a curb and went up onto a sidewalk a little, awakening to brake just in time to barely miss a light pole. My Dad used to tell me about how in his youth he would regularly drive while intoxicated, falling asleep at the wheel. He would see a huge brick wall in his sleep, which made him brake and wake up, preventing him from crashing the car.

When my son Matthew was one year old, just barely beginning to walk, he fell face-first directly onto a piece of metal that had a sharp edge. The metal piece punctured and tore the skin right between his eyes, creating a gushing, gaping wound immediately above his nose. Smack dab in the center of his eye line, right between his two big beautiful blue eyes. If the metal had hit a quarter-inch to the left or right, he probably would have lost an eye. If it had penetrated one half-inch deeper than it did, it probably would have caused skull or brain injury. It may have even killed him. The E.R. physician marveled that night, at how "lucky" this kid was. "Oh, he's not lucky," I said. "God is watching over him. God protected him tonight; I am certain of that!" The position of that wound was just too perfect to be anything *but* supernatural protection. I hope that the scar on Matthew's face will always remind him that God and His angels have his back!

Prayers for protection are powerful! God is listening! "The gracious hand of our God is on everyone who looks to Him!" (Ezra 8:22 NIV) If you have experienced incredible physical protection at some point in your life, thank God for His guiding hand and steady eye upon you! Could it be that your "close call" was not a lucky break at all, but the undeniable evidence of a caring, loving Father Who desired to shield you from danger?

Consider how His shielding arm has been revealed to you. Consider also how He might wish to use you to help others to safety in Him. As the outstretched fingers of the Lord, we can touch endangered lives with fearless faith in a fearless God. We can demonstrate victory over fear, and use that testimony to lead others out of their own fears. We can pray protection over our kids, knowing He will hear and answer according to His will.

How wonderful it is to dwell in His safety!

> *"If I make my bed in the place of the dead, or*
> *dwell in the uttermost parts of the sea,*
> *even there shall Your hand lead me, and*
> *Your right hand shall hold me."*
> *Psalm 139:8-10 (Amplified)*

CHAPTER 20

ARMS OF DELIVERANCE

"Deliver me, O Lord, from my enemies. I flee to You to hide me."
Psalm 143:9 (AMP)

Psalm 91 is the best anti-fear remedy I've ever applied in my life. I read it often. But not because of spiders and stalkers. Its words have protected me from far more real threats that seek to destroy my very life on a daily basis.

They are the spirits of darkness. Soldiers of evil.

They are my enemies.

I used to say, rather matter-of-factly and with a pinch of pride, that I didn't *have* any enemies. But I was only thinking about *human* enemies. I would read the Psalms and think, "Wow, David sure had a lot of enemies! Why did so many people hate him?" It did not occur to me that I, like David, have full armies of *spiritual* enemies who hate me and want to ruin me. When I realized this, I figured out that the Psalms are chock full of ammunition to use against the demons that torment me in this life. David knew the forces plotting against Him were spiritual forces (not all human), and that the same God protecting Him physically could protect

Him in the spiritual realm. Sure, I may have no *human* enemies (to my knowledge), but since before my mother even gave birth to me (while yet in her womb), I've had enemies in the spirit realm. They are 100% evil and 100% out to get me! *Now* when I read the Psalms, I relate to David's words much more closely. Because I have seen the worst enemies imaginable, at work in my own life. I am very aware of their presence. While I remain ever cautious, watchful, wary-- I am not afraid of these enemies. God has given me victory over them.

ENTRIES AND STRONGHOLDS OF EVIL

My first up-close, audible and visible encounter with demons was in a church meeting in Anchorage, Alaska. Reverend Bob Larson (pastor, teacher, author of several books and founder of Spiritual Freedom Church) had come from Denver, Colorado to our church, to do a teaching workshop about evil influences at work in our world.[1] At first, I didn't want to go to the event. I'd watched a few videos of Bob Larson conducting exorcisms on people. And although I was astounded by the power of God to evict the demons from their sufferers, I lacked understanding of how that all worked. It scared me. *Where do the demons go when they leave a person? Could they enter me?* I was a few months pregnant with our first child at the time. I remember thinking, "I don't want to risk our baby getting demonized if I go to this meeting." I knew so little then compared to what I know now. My fears were, like the spider tree, completely imagined, based on nothing real. But they were real to me.

Mark educated me enough to ease my apprehension about being at the workshop. He understood "spiritual warfare" much better than I did at that point. He explained to me that during an exorcism, Bob Larson always ordered the demon(s)- in Jesus' name- to go to the pit of torment. There was nowhere else they could go; they *had* to obey the order given them in Jesus' name. Mark had read some of Bob Larson's books and had followed his ministry closely for quite some time. He assured me it was spiritually "safe" to go to the meeting. I reluctantly agreed to go and help out, to pray with people or to work at the book table afterward. "But if things get too weird, I'm leaving!" I said.

Now I know that I was *supposed* to be at that meeting. And I was a fool to be afraid! I had nothing to fear with the power of Christ in me!

That night, people had come from many different places to hear the teaching about evil. Some, like me, came with skepticism or even with intent to criticize what Bob Larson would do there. Some came because they thought (or knew) they might have a demon, and they needed help. They needed ministry. They needed freedom from evil's bondage.

The teaching emphasis that night was "Entries of Evil and Pulling Down Strongholds". We sang a new song about pulling down strongholds in the name of Jesus. I didn't even know what a stronghold *was* at that point. But I still sang along, eager to come into new knowledge. That night began just like most church services begin. After the time of singing and an opening prayer, Pastor Bob began to teach from the Bible. He cited so many Scriptures that I had trouble keeping up in my notebook. He taught about some of the primary ways that evil spirits enter a person's soul, with soul destruction as their goal.

Before that time, I thought that demon spirits would only really torment a person if he had directly "brought it on" himself somehow, through heinous acts, habitual "really bad" sins, or involvement with the occult. If I stayed away from Satanic death metal, ouija boards, voodoo dolls, horoscopes, and tarot cards- I'd probably be out of demonic reach, right? *Wrong!* That was a lie I believed! I have since come to understand that *absolutely no person is out of Satan's reach.* No one is immune to his schemes. Even Jesus was deliberately tempted in His life, multiple times, by the prince of the power of the air. (I wonder how many more times Satan tempted Jesus, beyond just what we read about in Scripture.)

The devil is a bully who tries to ensnare *everybody* in his sin trap. He keeps trying until he finds our weaknesses, until he finds an "in". The work of his evil *does* operate through occult activity; that is for certain. But that's just *one* of the ways evil can gain entry into a life. As I have learned because of the work and ministry of Bob Larson and others at Spiritual Freedom Church (Portland)[2], evil also operates in other ways, such as:

- abuse- *physical, emotional, or sexual trauma committed against you*
- abandonment- *a loved one leaving you or rejecting you*
- inheritance- *a cursed bloodline (because of your ancestors' sins)*
- willful sin- *consciously, continually choosing to do something you know is wrong according to the Bible*
- addiction- *habitually defiling God's temple with idolatry in the form of destructive "bad habits"*

Notice that several of these are not even "chosen" by the affected person. They are involuntary. The result of *other* people's sin. The sin of others can still work against a person spiritually, as much as his own sin can. Sin has a domino effect. One person gets knocked down by another's poor choices. He proceeds to knock others down because of what was done to him. And those knock others down, and the process continues. Like a chain reaction. Before long, everyone's knocked down- because of that initial sin act. It's so *destructive!* THIS IS HOW THE DEVIL OPERATES. It goes far beyond the work of the occult. It's at work in our "normal" everyday lives.

So even if your exposure to the occult has been little to none (as mine has been), you are not "safe" from the devil's work- except through Christ and the Word of the Lord. Spirits of evil want to draw you and me away from the truth of the Lord. They want to afflict us in our inner selves (Psalm 143:12)-- to inflict painful soul wounds caused by sin. They want us living in all of sin's bondage, forgetting God and denying His love and promises. The unrelenting influence of evil can horribly torment a person in his soul. David described how this feels, in Psalm 143:3 (AMP): *"The enemy has pursued and persecuted my soul! He has crushed my life down to the ground and made me to dwell in dark places as those who have been long dead."*

Our enemies find their way into our souls and then their affliction remains and worsens over time as they gain their sturdy footholds- strongholds of evil- in us. *Common strongholds are anger, fear, rejection, and self-hatred.*

The night of the Bob Larson meeting, I caught a glimpse of this torment of soul. Not in my own soul. (That would happen years later.) But I saw it in others. It was an emotional anguish that turned my stomach and made me weep with compassion for its victims.

After his time of teaching, Pastor Bob asked everyone in the room to consider where they might have been vulnerable to the entry of evil in their lives. He asked them to go to the point of the pain where that entryway was opened. To go back in their memory, back to the exact time and place where their soul wound was inflicted. As they did this, men and women all over the room began to cry. Some sobbed loudly, while others silently sat in stillness, working through that point of pain where they'd been hurt. Bob asked those who'd been sexually abused in some way to stand up and receive prayer. *I could not believe how many people stood up.* Many women were standing, crying. And some men, too. It was sickening to see so openly the effects of our enemy being played out in these people. But they were standing ready to cast off the shame they'd borne for far too long. One of them was my friend Anna. A girl I worked with, hung out with. A girl I cared about.

I gasped to think that my sweet, kind, Godly friend had been hurt in this way. *No, not Anna! How could they?* Then I started crying.

My heart was broken and racing as I hurried over as fast as I could to lay my hand on Anna and pray for her to be free of her pain. Pastor Bob came over and prayed aloud with her. Then he led Anna- and all others standing- through a series of steps to forgive their abusers and to give the pain and their abusers over to Jesus.

They were asked to visualize themselves in that moment of the abuse act, then to forgive their offender all the way, then to move safely away from their offender while holding the hand of Christ, as He forgave the offender and took that sin act on Himself.

That was one of the most beautiful moments in my walk with the Lord up to that point. I had never been in a church meeting where this was done! This was real, nitty-gritty, we're-not-messing-around-anymore *ministry*. The way Jesus did ministry. I watched in thankful prayer as people all around me went to the point of their pain, forgiving their offenders, turning their offenses - and the resulting suffering- completely over to Jesus. Jesus' resurrection power was very alive and obvious to me in those moments. I stood in awe of it, watching as He restored all these tormented souls *back to wholeness* in Him!

I stayed at the side of my friend, who now was smiling through her tears. Her shoulders had been hunched over, but were now relaxed as she openly praised the Lord for leading her to that meeting that night. Anna and I stood hugging for several minutes, and she told me she felt the highest degree of relief she had ever experienced since the time of her molestation. She felt *clean*.

WOW! HALLELUJAH!! We praised God together and stood in amazement over what had just happened.

A few other people in the sanctuary, however, were not so quick to receive healing. They were staring angrily at Bob, with looks of hatred in their eyes. A few yelled out at him, saying, "I hate you!" Some snarled or even growled, like animals. I heard someone cry out, "You can't have him! You'll *never* have him!" Mark and several other men moved quickly to forcefully restrain a man who had lashed out in vengeful anger toward Pastor Bob, until Bob could get over to him. This man obviously was overtaken with a demonic spirit (or several). Bob used his Bible to physically bind the man's hands and arms behind his back. *Invisible handcuffs.* Bob had to bind the man that way in order to talk to him and minister Christ's deliverance to him. He would send the man's demons to torment. They were completely powerless against the

Word of the Lord. Once their legal rights were renounced in the courts of heaven, they had no spiritual right to be there and no foothold anymore. They had to go! And go they did.

By the time the meeting ended, Pastor Bob had ministered to several more people just like that man. He identified what legal rights the demons had to enter those people. Then he cast the demons out and sent them- in Jesus' name- to the pit of torment! It was incredible to see the change in the afflicted people. It was miraculous. I have seen it several times since, in various settings, and it never gets old-- seeing how Jesus sets the captives free and transforms them from the inside out! Their whole facial expression changes, from a shameful anger to a joyful peace. Their voices calm, their muscles relax. They are changed, just like the demoniacs Jesus healed! (Mark 5, Matthew 8) I have never seen a person freed of a demon who did not _immediately_ give praise to Jesus for releasing him from that captivity.

That night at the church, we all felt like praising Jesus awhile, before going home. So we had a time of worship. We sang the song about pulling down strongholds. Only this time I knew _exactly_ what I was singing about. I could not contain my tears; the love in my heart swelled so big as I thanked Jesus for all He had done to free us from our enemies.

I would witness many more similar victories in the coming years, talking with people who needed to return to the dreadful point of their pain, forgive their offenders, and be liberated by Jesus Himself. I would never again shy away from waging war against our tormenters. I saw the _power of Jesus_ to defeat them.

It was a good thing I realized that I was a partaker of that power. Because I would need to rely on it years later, to defeat demons trying to take over my own heart.

MY EGYPT

When the children's movie _The Prince of Egypt_ was released in theaters, I went to see it on the big screen.[3] By the end of the opening song, *Deliver Us*, [4] tears were already dripping down my face. The lyrics were so meaningful to me. Because I knew the story wasn't just about the Hebrew slaves working in harsh conditions in Egypt hundreds of years ago. The song was about me. And you. *Everyone* in this world. The song of the slaves was a familiar prayer I had also prayed to God, on days when the evil of this world had gotten too heavy for me to bear. *Deliver Us* sings of the whip stinging a shoulder. The toil, the sweat, the darkness and despair that enslavement brings. It is a cry for help, a plea to be heard. A seizing of hope for a better life in a better place. I had been a slave to my own anger, my fears, my self-hatred, the hurt that tried to steal my spiritual freedom daily. **But God.** God was delivering me from *all* of that. He is still delivering me. Sometimes on hard days, I sing that deliverance song. I plead for rescue, as the Israelites did in Egypt:

> *Deliver us out of bondage to the Promised Land.*
> *Send a Shepherd to shepherd us!*

Hearing that song for the first time, being stricken by all it symbolized in my own life, I knew my Shepherd had already come. To watch over me. To lead me to His safe place of promise. To keep the wolves away.

But sheep are not the smartest of creatures, and sometimes they wander off. They get lost for awhile. Then they are more susceptible to their predators. This happened to me recently. I didn't stay near enough to my Shepherd Jesus. I strayed. And before long, I fell into a pit of self-pity. I was met in the pit by several spirits who would tempt me to deny the Truth I had cherished my whole life. And I wouldn't resist them completely at first...

I had been hurt and was grieving loss again. Although Mark had not harmed me physically (and never has), I felt the *internal* blow of some decisions he made, decisions I disagreed with. Decisions that affected me but that I had no control over. And although Mark had not been unfaithful to me sexually, I felt betrayed, like my heart was shattering into a million pieces. Grief's darkness overtook me in such a way that I did not think I could ever recover. I felt as though I'd lost a child. I felt as though a big part of me *died*. My heart was hardened toward Mark worse than I thought it ever could be. I had no pity for him this time, no grace to give. I took back my forgiveness. That well dried up. I began dwelling in anger and -without noticing- I became enslaved to it.

And so, I started giving place again to that imaginary life which I had chosen to renounce two years earlier. Only *this* time, instead of stifling the thoughts of a different life, I savored them.

My former prayers of, "Lord, help me love Mark like You do" turned to, "Lord, help me *not hate* him". But, like I said before, it's completely ineffective to ask God to take away an emotion that you keep choosing for yourself. Why pray something gone that you don't really *want* gone?

The fact is, I was choosing hatred. I hated Mark for what he had done.

Hate can consume (and destroy) a person *quickly*. It's not an emotion that is easily turned off, once turned on. Once I chose it, hate grew in me at an alarmingly rapid pace, opening my heart's door to something even uglier- to the offspring of hate, which is murder. Before long, I wanted <u>death</u> for Mark.

In those prior years when Mark wanted to die and prayed for God to take him, I had pleaded with God to spare him. But now, I was different. I had given in to darkness and become apathetic. I didn't care if Mark lived or died. I thought I'd probably be better off if he *did* die. In my heart I was just like Job's wife who told her husband to "curse God and die". Even though I didn't *want* to curse God, in my heart I was telling Mark, "Die!" I no longer cared about his life. And I justified these thoughts, saying, "I can't help it. This is how I feel. Look what <u>he</u> has done..." *I blamed Mark for my own wrong choices.* Just as Adam blamed Eve in the Garden of Eden. I blamed my spouse's actions for my own sin. My heart had progressed from forgiving to angry, then to hateful, then murderous. In a very short time.

I had allowed myself to be tied up once again. Death-embracing instead of life-giving. Mean-spirited instead of joyful. Vengeful instead of gracious and merciful. Once again enslaved to the influence of evil.

But it didn't take long for God to shake me back to my senses.

ASSOCIATING WITH GOMER

God had to wake me up to the darkness I was giving place to. Through a Bible study I was doing on my own, He led me to a story I knew very little about. This was not a story I had heard in Sunday school or vacation Bible school. I could not remember ever hearing it in church. It's too "weird"- too adult and dark- for most Sunday morning services. But God led me straight to it at the very time in my life when I needed a major "slap upside the head"! The wake-up call I needed came in the story of Hosea and Gomer.

Hosea was a prophet, a righteous man of God. In obedience to God, Hosea took for his wife a woman of loose morals, named Gomer. Gomer was known as a harlot in her community. She had taken multiple lovers even before Hosea married her. And then, once they were married, she cheated on Hosea with multiple sex partners. She bore three children, none of which Hosea was father. Her infidelity brought shame upon Hosea and his family. Before long, she left Hosea. (Notice it was not the other way around!) Hosea had cared for Gomer, giving her a faithful, caring, safe environment in which to live. But she had made idols out of her other lovers. Thinking she would have a better life with them, she left. But she ended up desperate, forsaken by society, with no way to make a living but through slavery.

It is unclear whether Gomer ended up a sex slave, but many scholars believe that's probable. A woman like Gomer would have likely been mistreated and used on many levels by those who had purchased her and made her their slave. Bound by her captors, Gomer's reputation seemed forever marred. It seemed she would die a slave. *But Hosea bought her back.*

In faithful obedience to God, Hosea went to Gomer's captors and paid them to release her. He paid for the freedom of this unfaithful, prostituting woman who had betrayed him and left his side. Just as Jesus gave His life to redeem unfaithful us and save us from the pit of torment, Hosea restored Gomer back to wellness and freed her from her captors, despite her foolishness. WOW.

The Bible says that God's whole purpose in all of this was to give a clear representation of what He has done for His people, the unfaithful ones He loved. What a powerful correlation this holds for us today.

What God showed me through all of this is that *we* are the adulterous ones who place idols above Him. We reject His pure and perfect love for our own foolish wantonness. We turn from His Word to our own selfish desires, thinking everything will be alright. But before long, we end up in a dark, scary place- chained up by enemy spirits and regretting our sin. But Jesus with His blood has bought us back! He offers us unconditional acceptance even after we have been unfaithful to Him with multiple idols, our "other lovers".

Gomer's story got my attention and made me realize that my desire for a different life (apart from Mark) was a type of spiritual adultery that I was committing against God. I had again rejected His higher love and self-sacrifice that I'd been called to so clearly, many times earlier. I needed deliverance from the bondage of my own flesh.

One night I spent a long time praying- on my knees and in tears- meditating on the book of Hosea and all that it told me. I was ashamed of myself but also so aware of the freedom that Jesus would bring to me if I was willing to break free of my flesh. I remembered what my friend Anna had done years before, in that Friday night church meeting back in Alaska. And so I did the same thing. I went to every point of pain where I felt Mark had betrayed me. I forgave him in my spirit, with Jesus looking on- and then I gave that hurt to Jesus and stepped away from it, holding Jesus' hand.

I did this in a room alone with Jesus.

I had no "counseling", no other person or friend around me who knew what was going on in me. *It was just me and God.*

And then that night, like Hosea undoubtedly did for Gomer, Jesus took my shackles off, cleaned me up, gave me clean clothes to wear. He nourished me and led me back into a pure and selfless love. *The foul spirits of hate and murder lost their footholds in me that day! Jesus had single-handedly delivered me from that darkness.* I was clean again, relieved--- just like the people I had seen freed of their demons. And all I could do was thank Him and praise Him. I was reconciled back to Christ. And in that reconciliation, I turned once again to forgiveness. To mercy, to grace. To LOVE. My marriage relationship was restored to purity and made strong and healthy once again. This was a miracle of grace. I cared about Mark's life again. I cared about his future.

Jesus freed me to be the pure bride I was meant to be.

The sweet revelation of God's redemption.

THE ARMOR AND THE SWORD

The evil in this world is indeed greater and more powerful than we are. Without Christ, we cannot defeat it. I and others I know have tried to defeat evil apart from Jesus. It never works out. The reason for this is that we have something in common with evil spirits. *But Christ doesn't.* (Mark 5:7) Unlike us, Christ never gave in to the pressure of His enemies- the pressure to turn from the will of His Father. Christ's righteousness gives Him the dominion over Satan and his demons. The power we have inherited in Him is the power of His righteousness. His wholeness can "bind the strong man" (Satan) and stop him from robbing us of all the joys Jesus came to give us! (Mark 3:27) We fit the description in Psalm 107, which says, *"They cry to the Lord in their trouble, and He delivers them out of their distresses. He sends forth His Word and heals them, and rescues them from the pit and destruction."* (Psalm 107:19-21 AMP)

Ephesians 6 speaks of drawing from God's strength- which

knows no bounds- and putting on His armor. Armor we can gird daily to protect us from the work of these tireless enemies. Personal Protective Equipment ("PPE") in the spiritual realm! You can continually put on the pieces of His armor, reminding yourself that you are at war with evil, and you are called to overcome it with good. DAILY. Put on the helmet of salvation. The breastplate of righteousness. The shield of faith. The belt of truth. The sandals of peace through the Gospel of Jesus. Wear them with confidence and fearlessness!

The only *weapon* mentioned in Ephesians 6 is the Word of the Lord. Because it's the only one we need! It's the Sword of the Spirit of God. It's the only weapon Jesus used against the devil in the wilderness. And it was *enough*! It is not correct to say, "There's power in the Word of God". It's more accurate to say, "The Word of God *IS* power!" It will hurt our enemies every time we use it against them! They hate its truth. It sends them straight to their doom. That's why it is so vitally important that we read it, study it, *immerse ourselves in it* when we are under attack or when we are allowing ourselves to be vulnerable by forgetting to don our God-given armor.

In your times of moral weakness and combat with demons, the Word of God will comfort and guide and strengthen you. It will make your enemies flee from you as you wield its truth against them!

Never underestimate the power that is the Word of God.

SOZO CHARA!

Two Greek words in Scripture have become meaningful banners of spiritual victory in my life. The verb "sozo" (translated "deliver" in English) is used in the New Testament to convey a *rescue*. It means to save from danger, to restore to a renewed state, to protect and make whole. The word "chara" means joy and gladness, the cause or occasion of one's rejoicing. These words have come together to define me in the experiences described in this book. These isolated moments- these *encounters* with the Lord God of heaven- have something in common. They are ALL times when God has rescued me from very real danger, and restored me to wholeness in His love. Someday I want a sweatshirt custom-made with the words "sozo chara" across its front. If people ask me what it means, I will tell them my story. I will tell them that the cause of my joy- the occasion for my rejoicing- is every time He has freed me from the hand of my great "invisible" enemies, bringing me to the hiding place of safety where I know I am loved.

The occasions of rejoicing (my "chara's") were the times when He rescued me ("sozo'd" me). Because of Him, I have been freed from:

- *self-hatred*
- *self-pride*
- *jealousy and hatred toward women*
- *fear of an uncertain future*
- *a hopeless death*
- *fear of men's evil acts*
- *spirits of hate and murder*
- *anger*
- *unforgiveness*
- *doubt*

I will have more and more of these encounters until He takes me up to be with Him. He will free me of more strongholds until I am made perfect in His presence! He will do this for you, too! What evil has taken root in *your* life? What evil do you need Him to deliver you from now? From what bondage has He already delivered you? Go tell your story! *Tell others* how He has freed you!

Erwin McManus, author of *Chasing Daylight*,[5] has said that "*Star Wars* and *Avatar* are better stories than the ones many of us are telling with our lives." How true that is! What narrative are we telling to the world? Is it one of defeat, despair, pointlessness, vanity? Or is it one of glad victory, power, *triumph*? McManus has also said that "it's not hard to bring people to Jesus when you just *help them see Jesus in their story.* They will see their story and they will see God in it." That is what I have tried to do with this book. I have tried to tell you a great story. A *true* story, the best one I could tell you. But also to encourage you to **tell *yours*!**

Your story- so unique, so special- is also a revelation story. If you have chosen to see Jesus in it, it will be a sweet, amazing story you will be thrilled to tell- for the rest of this life and all of the next. It will be one with an unforgettably miraculous, happy "ending"- that really isn't an ending at all.

Your story is your legacy. It will last through eternity. Make it one of deliverance. Of redemption. Make it about Jesus.

"There is joy among the angels of God over one wicked person who repents- changes his mind for the better, heartily amending his ways, with abhorrence of his past sins." Luke 15:10 (AMP)

CHAPTER 21

HANDS TO HOLD FOREVER

"He tends His flock like a Shepherd.
He gathers the lambs in His arms and
carries them close to His heart."
Isaiah 40:11 (NIV)

It was after 4:00 p.m. on a Friday afternoon. "I gotta get out of here," I thought, as I packed up my things and prepared to leave my classroom and head downtown for a counseling appointment at 5:00. I'd learned about a counseling agency where I could receive Christian counseling without having to pay. That was a great thing, because I had no money to pay a counselor at the time. But I felt I really needed counseling. I needed to talk to somebody- someone I did not already know or work with. I needed to pour my heart out and be heard by an objectively listening ear. I needed *advice*. Maybe I just wanted to complain a little bit (or a lot?) about the way things were going at home. About how worn down I was from bearing the burden of pain with Mark, from bearing the weight of our financial struggles and juggling everything along with the physical and spiritual needs of our children. I was having difficulty being patient and reacting to problems in a Godly way. Maybe sympathy was what I wanted that day. Or just a new friend - someone who could see my situation from the outside and offer some pointers on how to persevere like a good soldier.

Exhausted but expectant, I drove to the building where my appointment was to take place. The Academy building in Vancouver. It's a grand old building with a rich history. This was to be my first session. I had made the appointment several weeks earlier; that particular day was the soonest they could meet with me. "I'm so glad I can _finally_ talk to somebody who will understand," I thought as I pulled in to the parking lot and then walked through the building entrance. I took the rickety old antique elevator up one floor to the room where my counselor would surely be awaiting my arrival, with a smile, a tissue box, and two ears ready to listen to my tale of woe.

I knocked on the door, but no one appeared to be on the other side of it. The air was tranquil; I heard no rustling or speaking. No shuffling of chairs or feet. I knocked again. Nothing. I called the number and got an answering machine. I left a message. It probably sounded something like, "Hi, I'm Davida and it's 5:00 on Friday. I'm here for my counseling appointment. _Where are you_?" And then I decided to wait a few minutes. "Maybe the counselor is late and doesn't have a way to call me," I thought.

So I waited. And waited. I was not feeling patient at all after about 10 minutes. After 20, I grew angry. "Just my luck!" I thought. "Why tonight? Why _now_? I really _have_ to talk to someone or I'm seriously going to LOSE my HEAD!"

I already had been feeling that unraveling, for weeks now, that steady coming-undone feeling where you feel you'll burst at the seams if _one_ more thing goes wrong.

I walked down the hall to where a man was working in another small office. "Hello, sir, excuse me...but do you know anyone who works over in the counseling agency down the hall?" I asked. "They're not in there, but I had a 5:00 appointment."

The man in the office smirked at me with a careless grin I did *not* appreciate. He looked at me in disbelief that I was even asking him such a question. "Na, I don't know. Sorry, lady- I can't help you." He said "I don't care" with his whole face before he turned around, putting his back to me, and began working again.

I don't know why the explosion came then, but it did. That man, showing no concern whatsoever for me, snubbing and turning his back on me like he did, was just the last straw. I am sure he didn't notice my gasping for air as I turned and headed straight for the women's restroom across the hall. But he may have heard my broken crying a moment later. I couldn't control the outburst of emotion I felt. There in the old bathroom (which I had to myself), I stepped into a stall, locked it, and stood against the cold tile wall just sobbing my heart out. *Why had my counselor not been there? Why had that man been so rude to me? Why had God allowed me to make all the arrangements to come here, when it would be a fruitless time that didn't help me at all?* I needed real help! I felt I had nowhere else I could go that night, for the kind of help I needed. I felt desperate, anxious. And pretty ticked off.

It took me quite awhile to calm down in the bathroom. But I eventually did. I washed my face and walked out trying to act like nothing had happened. The man in the office had left for the day. *Thank goodness I don't have to face him again!* Everything was quiet and closed up. I felt like I was the only person in that whole big building. By the time I got to my car, I was bawling again. It was like I had mustered just enough strength to get from the bathroom to the parking lot.

It had started raining pretty hard and had grown quite cold and blustery in the time I'd been inside the building. I turned on my headlights and windshield wipers and began the drive home. I was so angry and frustrated, so hurt and alone, that it was difficult to see the road through my tears and emotional state. I didn't really want to show up at home in my troubled state. *"Pull it together, Davida!"*

I pulled in to a nearby gas station and parked the car in a dark area where no one was around. Burying my arms against the steering wheel, crying uncontrollably over what had happened, I cried out, "God, why this disappointment now? Why? *Don't You CARE about me at all?* Don't you see I have nobody to talk to about everything?"

And then it hit me.

He wanted me to talk to *HIM*! Duh! Here I was crying out to Him about how alone I was-- but I wasn't alone at all! He was hearing me. And I heard Him whispering softly to me, "Talk to *Me*. I am your Wonderful Counselor! Your Prince of Peace."

Could it be that God had arranged this time to be alone with me, instead of my spending the hour with a stranger? Of course He had. Instead of spending time with a "new friend", I needed to spend time with an old Friend. The first and best Friend I ever had.

Mark won't expect me home for another 45 minutes at least, I thought, as I made the plan right then to talk to God about everything I would have told the counselor. I already had the list in my mind, of what I needed advice on--what I needed to "get off my chest". There was a whole lot of "stuff". Baggage to unpack. Feelings to sort through. And so, I started talking. Aloud. Right there in the car with the raindrops beating down on the car roof and windows. Right there in my little bubble of space where no one but He could fully know exactly what I was going through.

I cannot imagine a better counseling session! It was amazing. I could not get over the relief I felt as I sat there talking to God, just as I would talk to someone sitting in the passenger's seat next to me. The Lord ministered peace and hope to me there. He gave me a pep talk, a very much-needed one. Wonderful Scriptures flooded my mind, ones I needed to hear. It was an intimate time- just Him and me. An unexpected meeting with Someone Who had been wanting to speak to me as much as I wanted to speak to somebody. *I was in a place where I was ready to talk and listen-- to HIM.* The revelation I received in that 30-minutes span of time- there in my blue Hyundai- was truly incredible. God unveiled Himself as my Counselor that evening. I drove home, completely out of tears, not beaten down anymore, but feeling light and refreshed. I wasn't mad about that other counselor being a no-show. God showed up instead, and it was the best counseling session ever.

That was just one time out of *many*, when the Lord has shown me a glimpse of what eternity will be like with Him. Well, minus the tears and heartache. That will be all healed up. But, the resting on Him- the closeness of His hand to mine- the *intimacy*. He will not stand off at a distance from us- then OR now! He's as close as we let Him be!

That night was reminiscent of another night much earlier in my life, when I heard Jesus call me to be close to Him always. It was the night He asked me to be His beloved for all of my life... at a time when the future was wide open and staring me in the face...

About a month before I graduated high school, my Dad was asked to preach in our church. It was a small mid-week gathering in Alamo, Texas. The kind that isn't packed with people. I didn't know how much time my father had spent in preparation for speaking that night. I hadn't asked him what he'd be preaching about. But I knew whatever it was, it would come from his heart and would reflect the heart of God, because that's just how Dad was. He always spoke from his heart. And he made a habit of reflecting the heart of the One in Whose image he was made. It was his way. I'd heard my father preach many times, so I entered into the sermon time rather unexpectedly that night, ready to listen but feeling rather "ho-hum", knowing that I'd probably learn something, but having no clue that my heart was about to be opened, stricken, then re-molded for months to come, because of what I would hear that night.

Dad's message that night was about following Jesus. He asked, "What kind of Christ follower are you?"

Dad knew his audience. He knew he was talking to a group of people who already professed a relationship with Jesus. Just about everyone there had openly claimed to already be a follower of Jesus- even the kids in the room. But we'd not been asked recently, what KIND of followers we were. *Isn't there only one kind of Christ follower? You either follow Him or you don't, right?*

WRONG. As I would learn from Dad that warm April night in South Texas, a few different "types" of Christ followers are described in the New Testament. Six "categories" of followers, if you will.

THE MULTITUDES

First, there were *the multitudes* of people who followed Jesus during His time on Earth as a man. If you read about His life, you see that there were scores of people around Him much of the time, so many at times that they could not even be counted. He was followed- even chased and hounded- by the masses for a span of time during His earthly ministry. Sometimes great crowds thronged around Him, pressing in closely on Him from all sides (Mark 5:31). In Luke 12:1 there were so many thousands of people gathered near Jesus that they were trampling on one another! The scene may have been something like an overcrowded toy store two days before Christmas, or hundreds of young Beatle-maniacs storming a concert stage trying to get close to John Lennon or Paul McCartney.

The multitudes were the followers who would see Jesus from some distance away from where He was sitting or standing. They were the people sitting on the grass, or on the shore- somewhere near Him but not close enough to touch Him or to feel His breath on their faces. They knew Who Jesus was, but that did not mean they _knew Him_. "He was moved with pity and sympathy for them, because they were bewildered, harassed and distressed and dejected and helpless, like sheep without a shepherd." (Matthew 9:36 AMP) He knew they were lost without Him.

Some of the people in the multitude mob were following after Him for the wrong reasons. Maybe they followed Him to receive a free lunch, because they had seen Him supernaturally multiply food in His hands (John 6:26) and they really wanted to see that again. Maybe they followed Him not because of Who He was to them and how they could serve Him, but for what He could do for *them*. Their motives were rooted in selfish pursuits. Some of the multitude followers would hear Him and even see Him work a miracle and be devoted to Him for a time, but at some point would return to their "regular lives" and be seemingly unaffected by having been in His presence (John 6:66). This seems incredible considering the things He did, but is this really so hard to believe? How many of us have witnessed some mighty miracle of God in our lives, but still manage to go about our humdrum lives without letting the miracle truly seize hold of us and completely change us for the rest of our lives, so His wonders become all we think about and talk about? So often we don't want to be labeled as "radical" or "fanatic", so we just live a fairly complacent life for Jesus. We'll say He's done great things, but that's about as far as it goes for us, effectually wandering around seeking the Lord Jesus and acknowledging His presence, but not doing what He does, not serving, not asking Him *what He would have us do.*

THE 120

The second group of followers were the 120 numbered in the upper room in Acts chapter 1. Many of these people had seen the miracles of Jesus, but they had also seen Him after He rose from the dead. He'd appeared to them in ways that gave "unquestionable evidences and infallible proofs." (Acts 1:3 AMP) They had also just recently seen Him ascend into the sky, caught up in a glory cloud and carried away from their sight. These 120 people were gathered together, praying. I can imagine what all they felt. Wondering what exactly was going to happen next. Wondering what to do next. Wondering when they would see Jesus again. Waiting, watching, praying. These faithful followers were closer to the Lord Jesus than the multitudes had been. But the third group was even closer.

THE 70

The third group consisted of 70 special followers, described in Luke 10:1-11. These disciples were chosen, appointed, and sent out to places that Jesus was going to go. They were sent out to prepare His coming. He called them *lambs going into the way of the wolves.* Jesus gave them a list of things NOT to bring with them, for His provision would be proven. He told them not to get sidetracked. Their mission would be shown to them as they went. He told them to stay focused and to bless the people they encountered, telling them, "The Kingdom of God has come close to you!" (Luke 10:9 AMP)

These 70 followers were not given many specifics about what to do; they were just told to go. They were missionaries. Servants. Whole-heartedly acting out the will of Christ. Ready for what that would bring them.

THE 12

The fourth group of followers is a group you've heard of before. THE TWELVE. These were the twelve historically famous men selected specifically by Jesus to be His trainees. They had a very specific job to do, a special calling. And just like the 70 "missionaries" of Luke 10, they were equipped to do a very specific work. They were the ones who went with Him everywhere He went. They did as He did. They knew Him so well that they became like Him. They were disciples but also disciplers, learning how to teach others the ways of Christ after He was gone (II Timothy 2:2). They were closer to Him than the 70. But three of these were closer to Him than the other nine.

THE INNER CIRCLE

The fifth group was a small group, consisting of three disciples-Peter, James, and John. Of the twelve disciples of Christ, these three are mentioned the most in Scripture. They are often mentioned together and are called "the inner circle". They had a special closeness with Jesus, a marked bond that was strong. It stood out. They were always with Him! Sometimes these three were the ones that could go with Jesus when no one else could (Mark 5:37). These three had extra responsibilities because of their extra closeness with the Messiah. I believe Peter, James, and John experienced rich intimacy with Christ. When they went with Him up on a high mountain, He revealed a part of His glory to them that they had not seen-- His Transfiguration.

On the mountain, these three Christ followers saw Him glow. "His face shone clear and bright like the sun, and His clothing became as white as light." (Matthew 17:2 AMP) Moses and Elijah appeared there, talking to Jesus. And then a shining cloud of light came down, and from the cloud came a voice- the voice of God- saying, "This is My Beloved Son, in Whom I am well pleased; hear ye Him!" (Matthew 17:5 KJV) Then the disciples fell on their faces, afraid. But Jesus "came and touched them and said, 'Arise, and do not be afraid.' When they had lifted up their eyes, *they saw no one but Jesus only.*" (Matthew 17:7-8 NKJV) These three saw the glory of Jesus more than the other disciples and more than the 70 and the 120. But there is one more category.

THE ONE AT JESUS' BREAST

The last category is a category of one. "The disciple whom Jesus loved". John.

Of everyone Jesus knew and spoke with on a regular basis, John was the one who was always right with Him. He was the constant friend. The one who loved Him most consistently, even when others were betraying and denying Him. John was the one physically resting on Jesus. The one leaning up against His chest as they sat to break bread at the Last Supper. (John 13:23) What a comfort John was to Jesus, when He looked down at Him from the cross and saw him there with His mother! (John 19:26) He told John to take care of her, and *He knew that John would follow through.* John cared about what Jesus cared about. His love for Jesus was truly selfless. And when Jesus resurrected from the dead, John was the one who recognized Him right away, when Peter did not. (John 21:7) I believe that John knew Jesus more intimately than the other groups that followed Him. No wonder God showed John Himself so fully! (Read the book of Revelation!) No wonder John didn't die a martyr's death! His life ended the same way he lived it out...resting on Jesus' breast, *seeing the beauty of His glory.*

You know how some things you wish you could have on a video, so you could watch them again and again and kind of re-live them? That's how I feel about my Dad's sermon that night. Because I was <u>changed</u> that night. I was called to a deeper love for Jesus. By the end of that talk, I knew I wanted to follow Christ the way John did. I didn't want to be numbered with the multitudes, the 120, the 70, the 12, or even the three. *I wanted to be the one in the room resting my head right up on Jesus' chest.* I wanted to be one associating closely with His suffering. Recognizing Him in His glory light. Loving Him completely and not being satisfied with anything less than intimacy with Him.

This is what He wants from me! And He wants it from *you*, too. He wants closeness.

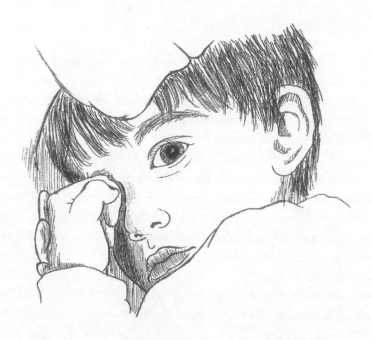

AND WE DANCE

Someone recently asked me, "Who is Jesus, to you?" For me, it was easy to answer that. He is so much to me. He's everything I've described in this story of mine. What I feel for Him is not only because of what I've read about Him in the Bible. It's not only what I've heard about Him from my parents or preachers. *He has shown Himself marvelously to me.* As my Lover. My Savior. My Maker. As my Deliverer. My Forgiver. My Healer. My Peace. He's my Protector. Provider. Rescuer. Redeemer. All the things I've shared with you in this book are just *some* of the times when Jesus showed me things about Himself. In otherwise common environments. My childhood bedroom. A college dorm room. A snowy highway. An ICU hospital room. A dentist's office. A patch of grass in front of an apartment complex. A living room couch. A blue Hyundai. A little church service in a small town. These are places where God's glory was uncovered before my eyes. His glory is my bright present *and* my bright future. His love is where I'm always accepted, always cherished, always safe.

Jesus has all the space and all the time for every one of us to love Him the same way that John loved Him. To be so close that you feel His breath. You recognize His voice. You know His touch.

If I asked you, "Who is Jesus to you?" what moments of your life would *you* think back to? What times and spaces have you known He was right there with you, loving you, keeping you in His hand? If this is a moment like that, call out to Him. Feel His warm embrace. Receive the comfort He brings.

Growing up, I never danced with any boy. As an adult, I still have never danced with a man. Not even with my husband. I've only ever "danced" with Jesus. It is something I do just with Him. In times of worship and private prayer, it's just me and Him, dancing together. His arms leading me, embracing me. His hands holding mine, healing me. I don't think dancing with anyone else could be any better than this anyway.

To dance with the Prince of heaven is to be steadied. To follow

His lead. To be so near Him that you hear His voice. To feel His breath, giving you life. To dance with eternal Love is to believe He has only your best on His mind. To trust He won't let you go. Ever. To have the overwhelming sense that you are home in His arms- that in His presence is where you belong now and always.

If we say we love Jesus intimately, but do not love others with His self-sacrificing, purer, higher love, then we are fools who do not really love Him at all. We are called to bear His light *so that others may see Him.* **We are instruments of His revelation!** We're His hands in a sin-soaked, love-starved world. He has called us to show forgiveness as He forgives. To love deeper and higher, as He loves. To minister healing and deliverance through His power, as He ministers. To speak truth as He *IS* truth. To give to others as He gives to us. It's not easy to live like Jesus lived. But living this way truly brings us close to His heart. So close that we hear His heartbeat. Then ours comes into synchrony with His. The arm of God reached *down* from heaven to Earth, and now reaches *out* to touch lives--through *us*. *This* is our purpose! *To dwell in His loving hand and to be the extension of it.* To be the outpouring of Christ- in our families, our marriages, our workplaces, our churches, our communities. Our world. Let's get a vision of heaven on Earth, and let's make it a reality wherever we can, with the way we live our lives.

The same arm that will rule the new heaven and the new Earth will hold you and me forever. (Isaiah 40:10) Our great delight in receiving any crowns from Him will be in laying them back down in adoration before His throne.

Jesus our Love, our Light, is worthy of ALL the glory and ALL the honor and ALL the praise. Forever and ever amen.

NOTES

CHAPTER 1

1   Miller, D. (2010). *A Million Miles in a Thousand Years: What I Learned While Editing My Life.* Nashville, Tennessee: Thomas Nelson, Inc.

CHAPTER 2

1   Harper, D. Online Etymology Dictionary. (2014). *"reveal".* Retrieved from http://www.etymonline.com/index.php?term=reveal
2   University of Washington: UW Courses Web Server. (2014). *Chapter 12: Optics and the Eye.* Retrieved from http://courses.washington. edu/psych333/handouts/coursepack/ch12-Optics_and_the_eye.pdf

CHAPTER 3

1   Purohit-Uchil, S. Complete Wellbeing. (November 19, 2013). *Saffron: Super Spice.* Retrieved from http://completewellbeing.com/article/ saffron-super-spice/
2   Raspin, S. eHow. (2014). *Reproduction of Flowering Plants Such As the Crocus & Gladiolus.* Retrieved from http://www.ehow.com/info_ 8589406_reproduction-plants-such-crocus-gladiolus.html

CHAPTER 4

1   Jeremiah 17:13 (KJV)
2   John 20:24-31

CHAPTER 5

1   Zeffirelli, F. (Director). (1977). Jesus of Nazareth [Television Mini-Series]. United States: National Broadcasting Company.
2   Gibson, M. (Director). (2004). *The Passion of the Christ* [Motion Picture]. USA: Newmarket Films.

CHAPTER 6

1   Genesis 2:16-17 and Genesis 3:2-3
2   Alcorn, R.C. (2004). *Heaven.* Wheaton, Illinois: Tyndale House Publishers.
3   Aten, D. (2007). Southwestern Medical Center. *Facts About Telomeres and Telomerase.* Retrieved from http://www4.utsouthwestern.edu/cellbio/shay-wright/intro/facts/sw_facts.html
4   University of Utah Health Sciences. (2014). *Are Telomeres The Key To Aging and Cancer?* Retrieved from http://learn.genetics.utah.edu/content/chromosomes/telomeres/

CHAPTER 7

1   II Kings 9:30-37
2   Acts 7:54-60

CHAPTER 8

1   Goldmann, B. (Producer), & Nelson, J. (Director). (1994). Corrina, Corrina [MotionPicture]. United States: New Line Cinema.
2   Giglio, L. & Tomlin, C. (2008). I Will Rise. On *Hello Love* [Audio CD]. Atlanta, GA: sixstepsrecords.

CHAPTER 10

1   Psalm 139:5 (AMP); Psalm 139:13 (NKJV); Psalm 139:16 (AMP);
    Psalm 139:17 (TLB)
2   Psalm 139:13-14 (NIV)
3   James 1:3-4 (Amplified)
4   Thornburg, A. (2014). Smithsonian National Museum of Natural
    History. *UV Rays Shed New Light on the Hope Diamond's Mysterious
    Red Glow*. Retrieved from http://mineralsciences.si.edu/research/
    gems/hope_diamond/blue_diamond_research.htm
5   BlueDiamondsUSA.com. (Date Unknown). Retrieved from http://
    www.bluediamondsusa.com/
6   *Famous, Historic, and Notable Diamonds*. Retrieved from http://
    famousdiamonds.tripod.com/portuguesediamond.html

CHAPTER 12

1   Genesis 8:13-21
2   Ingram, J. & Morgan, R. (2012). Forever Reign [Recorded by Hillsong
    Church]. On *Forever Reign* [Audio CD]. Sydney, Australia: Hillsong
    Music Australia.

CHAPTER 13

1   Cameron, J. (Producer & Director). (1997). *Titanic* [Motion
    Picture]. United States: Twentieth Century Fox Film Corporation
    & Paramount Pictures.
2   Harley, W. (2011). *His Needs, Her Needs: Building An Affair-Proof
    Marriage*. Grand Rapids, Michigan: Revell.

CHAPTER 15

1   Hall, M. (2007). Slow Fade [Recorded by Casting Crowns]. On *The
    Altar and the Door* [Audio CD]. Nashville, Tennessee: Beach Street
    Records.

CHAPTER 17

1 I Corinthians 15:52-53, Amplified
2 Revelation 21:4, NIV
3 Proverbs 4:22, NIV
4 Expected End Ministries. (2014). Retrieved from https://www.expectedendministries.com/
5 Souza, K. (November 20, 2013). *Healing Your Soul, Episode 1.* Retrieved from https://www.expectedendministries.com/media/index.cfm?page=watchkatie&media_id=65
6 Souza, K. (November 27, 2013). *Healing Your Soul, Episode 2.* Retrieved from https://www.expectedendministries.com/media/index.cfm?page=watchkatie&media_id=66
7 Souza, K. (November 27, 2013). *Healing Your Soul, Episode 2.* Retrieved from https://www.expectedendministries.com/media/index.cfm?page=watchkatie&media_id=66
8 Souza, K. (February 23, 2010). *The Glory Light of Jesus Part 4.* Retrieved from http://www.youtube.com/watch?v=vtBrFYi-ijs

CHAPTER 18

1 John 9:5, Amplified
2 Presson, S. (2014). CBN.com: The Christian Broadcasting Network. *What the Bible Says About Idols.* Retrieved from http://www.cbn.com/spirituallife/Devotions/Presson_KillIdols.aspx
3 Souza, K. (September 7, 2012). *Kingdom of the Son with Katie Souza, part 2 of 3.* Retrieved from http://www.youtube.com/watch?v=6Ep9YwkEnFQ

CHAPTER 19

1 Sallman, W. (1941). *Head of Christ.* [Original Painting].

CHAPTER 20

1 Bob Larson: DWJD Spiritual Freedom Church. (2014). Retrieved from https://www.boblarson.org/

2 Do What Jesus Did Portland. (2014). *Six Entries of Evil.* Retrieved from   http://www.dowhatjesusdidportland.org/deliverance/evil-entries.html

3 Chapman, B., Hickman, S., & Wells, S. (Directors). (1998). *The Prince of Egypt* [Animated Film]. United States: Dreamworks Animation.

4 Schwartz, S. (1998). Deliver Us. On *The Prince of Egypt.* [Soundtrack Recording]. Universal City, California: DreamWorks Records.

5 McManus, F.R. (2006). *Chasing Daylight: Seize the Power of Every Moment.* Nashville, Tennessee: Thomas Nelson, Inc.

ABOUT THE AUTHOR

Davida Blanton has studied the Bible independently all her life. She enjoys writing Bible devotionals and poetry. She also enjoys teaching, playing and listening to music, baking, and being near the ocean. Davida grew up on the Texas-Mexico border, where her parents were missionaries for over 20 years. She holds a bachelor of science degree in pre-med biology from Bob Jones University and a master of arts degree in teaching from Western Governors University. She currently teaches high school biology in Vancouver, Washington. *Sweet Revelation* is Davida's first published work. She hopes its readers will draw closer to God as they consider the visible touch of His hand on their own lives.

Printed in the United States
By Bookmasters